CONTROLLERSHIP

Update Service

BECOME A SUBSCRIBER!

Did you purchase this product from a bookstore?

If you did, it's important for you to become a subscriber. John Wiley & Sons, Inc. may publish, on a periodic basis, supplements and new editions to reflect the latest changes in the subject matter that you ***need to know*** in order to stay competitive in this ever-changing industry. By contacting the Wiley office nearest you, you'll receive any current update at no additional charge. In addition, you'll receive future updates and revised or related volumes on a 30-day examination review.

If you purchased this product directly from John Wiley & Sons, Inc., we have already recorded your subscription for this update service.

To become a subscriber, please call **1-877-762-2974** or send your name, company name (if applicable), address, and the title of the product to:

mailing address:	**Supplement Department** **John Wiley & Sons, Inc.** **One Wiley Drive** **Somerset, NJ 08875**
e-mail:	**subscriber@wiley.com**
fax:	**1-732-302-2300**
online:	**www.wiley.com**

For customers outside the United States, please contact the Wiley office nearest you:

Professional & Reference Division
John Wiley & Sons Canada, Ltd.
22 Worcester Road
Etobicoke, Ontario M9W 1L1
CANADA
Phone: 416-236-4433
Phone: 1-800-567-4797
Fax: 416-236-4447
Email: canada@wiley.com

John Wiley & Sons, Ltd.
The Atrium
Southern Gate, Chichester
West Sussex PO 19 8SQ
ENGLAND
Phone: 44-1243-779777
Fax: 44-1243-775878
Email: customer@wiley.co.uk

John Wiley & Sons Australia, Ltd.
33 Park Road
P.O. Box 1226
Milton, Queensland 4064
AUSTRALIA
Phone: 61-7-3859-9755
Fax: 61-7-3859-9715
Email: brisbane@johnwiley.com.au

John Wiley & Sons (Asia) Pte., Ltd.
2 Clementi Loop #02-01
SINGAPORE 129809
Phone: 65-64632400
Fax: 65-64634604/5/6
Customer Service: 65-64604280
Email: enquiry@wiley.com.sg

Controllership

The Work of the Managerial Accountant
Seventh Edition
2005 Supplement

Janice M. Roehl-Anderson

Steven M. Bragg

WILEY

John Wiley & Sons, Inc.

This book is printed on acid-free paper. ♾

Published by John Wiley & Sons, Inc., Hoboken, New Jersey.

Published simultaneously in Canada.

Library of Congress Cataloging-in-Publication Data:

Roehl-Anderson, Janice M.
Controllership, the work of the managerial accountant / Janice M. Roehl-Anderson, Steven M. Bragg. — 7th ed.
p. cm.
Updated ed. of: Controllership, the work of the managerial accountant / James D. Willson, 1999.
Published simultaneously in Canada.
Includes index.
ISBN 0-471-28118-2 (cloth : alk. paper); 0-471-67982-8 (supplement)
1. Managerial accounting. I. Bragg, Steven M. II. Willson, James D. Controllership, the work of the managerial accountant. III. Title.

HG4026.R645 2004
658.15'11—dc22

Printed in the United States of America

10 9 8 7 6 5 4 3 2 1

ABOUT THE AUTHORS

Janice M. Roehl-Anderson, MBA, is a partner with Deloitte, with over 20 years of consulting experience. She specializes in information systems security; financial and cost accounting system analysis, design, selection, and implementation; long-range information systems planning; and information management reviews/audits. She has also worked for US West. In addition to earning her BA in business at the University of Southern California, Jan has successfully completed the CPA exam, and has co-authored over 10 books, including *The Controller's Function: The Work of the Managerial Accountant.*

Steven Bragg, CPA, CMA, CIA, CPIM, has been the chief financial officer or controller of four companies, as well as a consulting manager at Ernst & Young and auditor at Deloitte. He received a master's degree in finance from Bentley College, an MBA from Babson College, and a bachelor's degree in economics from the University of Maine. He has been the two-time president of the 10,000-member Colorado Mountain Club, and is an avid Alpine skier, mountain biker, and rescue diver. Mr. Bragg resides in Centennial, Colorado. He has written the following books:

Accounting and Finance for Your Small Business (Wiley)

Accounting Best Practices, 3rd Edition (Wiley)

Accounting Reference Desktop (Wiley)

Advanced Accounting Systems (Institute of Internal Auditors)

Business Ratios and Formulas: A Comprehensive Guide (Wiley)

Cost Accounting: A Comprehensive Guide (Wiley)

Design and Maintenance of Accounting Manuals: A Blueprint for Running an Effective and Efficient Department, 4th Edition (Wiley)

Essentials of Payroll: Management and Accounting (Wiley)

Financial Analysis: A Controller's Guide (Wiley)

Just-in-Time Accounting: How to Decrease Costs and Increase Efficiency, 2nd Edition (Wiley)

Managing Explosive Corporate Growth (Wiley)

Outsourcing: A Guide to . . . Selecting the Correct Business Unit . . . Negotiating the Contract . . . Maintaining Control of the Process (Wiley)

Sales and Operations for Your Small Business (Wiley)

The Controller's Function: The Work of the Managerial Accountant, 2nd Edition (co-authored with Janice M. Roehl-Anderson, Wiley)

The New CFO Financial Leadership Manual (Wiley)

ACKNOWLEDGMENTS

With the rapidly changing business environment, it was essential that the material contained in this supplement be accurate, up-to-date, and relevant. Accordingly, in addition to the chapters written or revised by the two co-authors, these contributing authors, listed alphabetically, wrote or revised the chapters indicated:

Deborah Metzger, Manager
Deloitte, San Francisco, California
Chapter 41A, Maintaining and Upgrading ERP Financial Systems

Shinli H. Chi, CPA, Enterprise Applications, Senior Manager
Deloitte, Santa Ana, California
Ashlee Henry, Manager
Deloitte, San Francisco, California
Chapter 41B, Impact of Enterprise Applications on Finance

CONTENTS

Note to the Reader: Sections not in the main bound volume are indicated by "(New)" after the title. Material from the Seventh Edition that has been updated for this supplement is indicated by "(Revised)" after the title.

PREFACE

Though we have only just released the seventh edition of *Controllership*, we have issued this supplement to communicate a large amount of additional information that will be of immediate use to the practicing controller. Chapter 27, which covers the planning and control of receivables, has been substantially bolstered with new information about credit policies and procedures, the review and processing of credit applications, granting credit, creating and delivering invoices, collecting cash, and managing the credit and collections staff. In addition, the supplement includes a wide array of collection techniques, methods for managing payment deductions, and a discussion of the factors leading to a decision to outsource the collections function. All these topics have become increasingly important in light of tightening credit and rising interest rates.

Chapter 28, which covers the planning and control of inventory, has been enhanced in a similar manner. It now includes in-depth discussions of the best ways to conduct inventory purchasing, receiving, storage, picking, and shipping. Further, it delves into a variety of production issues that impact inventory levels. The chapter also describes a number of ways to collect and record inventory transactions, as well as control inventory quantity levels. The chapter concludes with a discussion of the alternatives to be considered when laying out a warehouse design to promote optimum inventory storage and movement. The intent of all these chapter upgrades is to give the controller a new set of tools to assist in reducing a company's investment in inventory.

We also felt that the expanded use of enterprise resource planning (ERP) systems called for entirely new chapters. Accordingly, Chapter 41A gives an overview of ERP financial systems, particularly in regard to maintaining and upgrading them. The chapter focuses on the current state of the ERP market, as well as what strategies to use to minimize costs while improving these systems. Chapter 41B addresses a key concern of the controller: How does an ERP implementation impact the accounting department? The impact is usually considerable, and this chapter frankly covers the pitfalls and altered risk profile caused by an implementation.

However, there is hope—we describe how to mitigate the risk with specific action items.

This supplement is intended to address the controller's most timely concerns, hopefully resulting in a reduced level of working capital investment and the avoidance of problems caused by an ERP implementation or upgrade.

Centennial, Colorado
Greenwood Village, Colorado
August 2004

PART 4

PLANNING AND CONTROL OF THE BALANCE SHEET

CHAPTER 27

PLANNING AND CONTROL OF RECEIVABLES

Pages 559–561. ***Replace Sections 27.1 and 27.2 with the following:***

27.1 INTRODUCTION (REVISED)

A simplistic view of the accounts receivable area is that a small detached group of clerks works in solitude to collect accounts receivable, mostly through phone calls. If this approach does not work, then intransigent customer accounts are turned over to a collection agency for more vigorous collection action. This approach may be used in some companies. However, close attention to better planning and control of a number of activities throughout a company will result in a significant reduction in its investment in accounts receivable, while at the same time reducing the proportion of bad debt losses. After reading this chapter, one will realize that the collection of accounts receivable really begins well before an invoice becomes overdue for payment, and requires close coordination between a number of departments.

This chapter addresses the organization of the credit-granting process, as well as techniques for making the best credit decisions. It then moves on to a discussion of improving the layout of invoices, as well as speeding their creation and delivery. We then cover the receipt and application of cash to open accounts receivable before moving on to the management and ongoing operations of the collection department, including the use of outsourcing. The chapter concludes with a discussion of measurement and control systems to ensure that the credit, billing, and collection functions are all operating properly.

27.2 CREDIT POLICIES, PROCEDURES, AND SYSTEMS (NEW)

The granting of credit to customers is the first point at which a company controls the size of its accounts receivable investment, as well as the number of bad debt problems it may eventually face. A company wanting to grow rapidly may elect to grant easy credit to nearly any customer who asks for it, and be willing to accept a greater degree of collection problems as a result. Alternatively, a company with a secure market niche and no particular desire to expand its market share may elect to pursue a tight credit policy, so there is minimal risk of any bad debt problems arising. If a company's products have very low gross margins, it may not have a choice in picking credit policies—any bad debt loss will result in the loss of such a high proportion of a product's price that it has no other choice than to only allow the tightest possible credit policy. The reverse is true if gross margins are high, giving a company the option to loosen its credit policy.

Company management must keep this general strategic vision in mind when creating a credit policy. This is an important document, for it defines the level of risk it is willing to take in granting credit, which can be itemized quite precisely, such as stating that accounts receivable are not to exceed 40 days. The policy also notes who is responsible for granting credit, so there are no turf battles (usually between the credit and sales managers) over who is allowed to do so. The policy can also describe the general criteria to be used to grant credit. This is useful for the sales staff, who can use it to predict the approximate level of credit the credit department is likely to grant its customers. Thus, the credit policy introduces a considerable degree of rigor to the credit-granting process, eliminating much of the confusion that can encompass this important function.

A company should review its credit policy from time to time. For example, it may find that changing economic conditions have resulted in a general decline in the ability of customers to pay their bills in a timely manner, so the credit policy must be tightened. Also, if the company is experiencing a high level of product obsolescence, the credit policy can be loosened for those products having declining sales, on the theory that the company may otherwise be forced to write off the inventory. The credit policy can also be varied by product line, since a company may have some products with a sufficiently high margin to allow some extra risk of noncollection, while the reverse is true for other product lines.

With a credit policy in place, the next step is to create a credit-scoring model. This can take a variety of forms, but is essentially a means for logically deriving a credit level to grant customers. It can be as simple as using the credit score recommended by Dun & Bradstreet in its "Credit eValuator" report, or one can build a model. Building a model can result in more accurate credit scores tailored to one's specific industry, though they can take a considerable amount of time to create and maintain. The components of a scoring model can include points granted for the number of years a customer is in business, the presence of professional managers instead of family members in management positions, positive cash flow, and the presence of a clean audit report. The number of points granted is then multiplied by the percentage of the customer's net worth to arrive at a dollar value of credit to be granted.

One can supplement the credit-scoring model with an early warning system that tells the credit department if a customer's financial condition is beginning to worsen. This information can come from a credit-reporting agency, or through an industry credit group, or even through such collection clues as a customer's no longer taking cash discounts or skipping selected invoice payments. If this information is processed and acted on promptly, one can restrict credit levels sufficiently quickly to keep from suffering significant credit losses.

With a credit-scoring and updating system in place, the next step is to establish a filing system for customer records. This should include a folder for each customer, containing its credit application, contact information, correspondence, and notations regarding any guarantees given by the customer. If there are guarantees or related loan documents, one should reference them only in the customer file and store the actual documents in a fireproof and locking cabinet for safekeeping. If there are many customer files or employees access them frequently, consider installing a document imaging system, where the original documents are scanned into a database from which they can be easily called up on anyone's computer. Though rather expensive, this approach improves the efficiency of the credit and collections staff, while keeping them away from source documents that might otherwise be misfiled.

With a storage system in place, one must now create documents to store in it. The main item is the credit application. This document requires each customer to list bank references, trade references, and identification information for both the owners and the company. In addition, be sure to include the following items to assist the company in making collections:

- *List multiple contacts*. A collector normally calls a customer's accounts payable department to resolve payment issues. If the result is unsatisfactory, it is most helpful to refer back to the credit application for a list of other contacts, such as the controller, chief financial officer, and president. These higher-level managers can frequently resolve payment issues.
- *Credit venue*. Require the customer to come to the company's state to resolve issues in court by using a credit venue provision. If the customer is a considerable distance away, the mere prospect of lengthy travel may induce an early settlement.
- *Personal guarantee*. Though customers are rarely willing to grant a personal guarantee of payment, it is worthwhile to add this provision to the credit application in hopes that some customers will sign it. If the signor has substantial assets, this can also result in the granting of a much larger credit line than would otherwise be the case.
- *Reimbursement of collection and NSF fees*. Include a requirement that the customer reimburse the company for all collection agency and legal fees incurred to collect from the customer. In addition, include a fixed fee for any "nonsufficient funds" (NSF) checks received from the customer, which should at least cover the bank fee charged to the company for every NSF check it submits to its bank.

If the credit department receives an application with some information not filled out, this is a sign that the customer may be trying to hide credit information. Not only should one return the application to the customer to have the remaining information completed, but also flag the customer as a potential credit risk right from the start, which should probably yield a lower credit line than would otherwise be the case.

The information included on a credit application is a snapshot of a customer's financial condition at a single point in time, and may not represent its condition even a few months later. However, one can estimate its financial condition by the timeliness of its payments for invoices on an ongoing basis. A problem arises when a customer does not place orders for lengthy intervals, since the credit department now has no recent history of payments on which to rely. A good policy that avoids this problem is to require customers to submit new credit applications if they have placed no orders in a long time. One way to introduce some rigor to the policy is to purge all customers from the accounting database if there have been no transactions with them for a fixed period, such as a year. Thus, when they attempt to place a new order and they do not appear in the accounting database, they are automatically routed to the credit department.

Once the credit department receives a completed credit application, it should process it with considerable speed. Otherwise, a customer will probably become impatient with the delay and take its business elsewhere, especially if it is attempting to process a rush order. The credit department may respond that it takes many days to receive a response from some references, and that this information is necessary to obtain a comprehensive view of a customer's credit situation. However, the underlying goal of the credit department is to find a way to assist the sales department in making a sale. Thus, the credit manager must monitor the time period required to process each application received and increase department resources as necessary to ensure that applications are completed in a timely manner.

A good way to increase the speed of application processing is through process centering. Under this concept, all application-processing tasks are given to one person, rather than being sequentially shifted among a number of people. By doing so, an application spends no time sitting in the work queue of each person involved in the process. If there are a large number of applications to be processed, then all the applications for a specific group of customers (such as those beginning with the letter *A*) will be given to one employee for processing, and so on.

Once the department grants credit terms, it is not sufficient to enter this information in the company's computer system and let the order entry staff proceed with an order. This approach results in the customer's not knowing the amount of its credit line, nor the company's standard payment terms, which can result in a great deal of payment confusion. Instead, a credit staff person should call the customer and explain the credit level and payment terms granted. This can even extend to the use of a written payment procedure that is sent to the customer, explaining exactly how the company processes invoices, when it expects payment, and how to apply for deductions. This high level of communication with customers tends to result in a reduced number of collection problems at a later date.

Once credit levels are granted and conveyed to the customer, the credit department's job is not yet through. It must continue to monitor credit levels. One of the easiest ways to do so is through the use of an exceeded credit line report. This report lists all customers whose orders have exceeded their credit limits, usually sorted in declining dollar order so the department can focus on the largest overruns first. By combining this information with a customer's payment history, the credit department can rapidly review the need for higher credit limits.

(a) PROCESSING CREDIT APPLICATIONS. The last section covered the policies, procedures, and systems used by a credit department. This section goes on to describe a variety of techniques for processing customer credit applications. The credit-granting process is driven by the volume of customers, the size of their orders, and the speed with which a credit review is needed. If orders are substantial, the credit department must expend a considerable effort in ensuring that it grants credit only where the risk of loss is minimized. Alternatively, a massive volume of new customers will completely bury the credit department, so some provision must be made for either automatically allowing or denying credit where order sizes are small.

A typical solution to the presence of many orders from new customers is to grant a small credit line with no credit review at all. Under this scenario, the cost of any potential bad debt is the same as or less than the cost of conducting a credit review, so the credit manager elects to avoid the review and just see which customers pay. If they build up a reasonable payment history and their order volumes subsequently increase, then a formal credit review will be in order.

The timing of customer orders can be a serious problem. For example, a salesperson lands a massive order and, sensing a major commission, puts intense pressure on the credit department to grant credit. Company management hears about the order and, wanting to achieve its revenue goal, also puts pressure on the credit manager. The result is a credit line far too high for a customer's finances, with the collections staff bearing the brunt of the inevitable late payment. A solution to this problem is having the sales staff discuss their sales prospects with the credit department in advance, giving the credit employees time to research the prospects in advance and let the sales staff know if their prospects will qualify for large amounts of credit. This approach calls for a considerable amount of communication between the sales and credit departments.

Collecting information about customers is a major part of the credit-granting process. The easiest way to obtain summary information is to purchase a credit report from either Dun & Bradstreet or Equifax. One can obtain reports from both companies over the Internet at www.dnb.com or www.equifax.com, respectively. Low-end reports (costing about $40) include identification information, such as a customer's primary place of business, the names of its officers, and its primary lines of business. A high-end report (costing up to $125) also includes information about each customer's payment history as well as the presence of any liens filed against its assets.

Another source of information is an industry credit group. These are groups of credit managers from related businesses that gather periodically to discuss the payment problems of their customers. Some maintain e-mail lists, so they can contact each other with fresh information about payment problems. A good source of information about industry credit groups is the National Association of Credit Managers (www.nacm.com).

If a customer is publicly held, it is also possible to access those financial reports that it is required to periodically submit to the Securities and Exchange Commission (SEC). These reports are listed on the SEC's web site at www.sec.gov. The most recent reports are quarterly 10-Q reports. Though they contain somewhat less information than the annual 10-K reports that public companies must also submit, there is still plenty of information on which to make credit decisions.

It may also be possible to visit a customer to obtain more credit information. For example, one can ask for a tour of the warehouse area and note the names of the customer's suppliers as listed on any stored items. These represent additional trade references to contact. One can also glean information from the general condition of the customer's facility, as well as the age of its equipment, all of which hint at its financial condition. Further, customers are more willing to show financial statements to a credit person who is on-site, as long as they return the statements before leaving the building. Finally, meeting customers begins to build a relationship, which is ideal for obtaining faster payments if this becomes an issue at some point in the future.

(b) GRANTING CREDIT. Once the credit department has all possible information about a customer, it needs to decide what level of credit to grant and what restrictions to put on the credit, if any. At worst, the credit staff may decide that a customer's financial condition precludes any credit at all. However, that does not mean that one of the customer's distributors might not have a looser credit policy. Thus, one alternative to credit is to refer a potential customer to a distributor.

If the credit department is willing to grant a small amount of credit, it can require cash in advance for the cost of the item being sold, and allow credit for the amount of the product's profit margin. This approach yields little risk and may still be better credit terms than a financially stricken customer could find anywhere else. The cash-in-advance terms noted here are substantially better for the company's risk position than cash on delivery (COD), since a customer could pay with a check for a COD item and then allow the check to bounce for lack of funds, which leaves the company in a worse position than if it had required cash in advance. Also, a customer can reject a COD delivery, in which case the company must pay the freight both going to and coming from the customer, which also increases its risk of damage in transit.

If the credit staff has withdrawn a customer's credit terms due to lack of payment, but the company offers such unique goods or services that the customer must continue to do business with it, an alternative for collecting any missing payments is to require a partial payment of the unpaid balance every time the customer places an order, which is to be paid on cash-in-advance terms. By doing so, a customer is forced to clear out its unpaid receivable balance over time. This is also a good way to determine a customer's long-term willingness to pay, which may eventually result in the granting of a small line of credit.

There are two types of guarantee that one can obtain to provide backup assurances that a receivable will be paid. One approach useful for smaller businesses is to obtain a personal guarantee; essentially, the company owner places his own assets at risk if the customer cannot pay the company. Wording to this effect is included in many credit applications, though customers usually look for it and cross it out when found. A problem is that the owner may have personally guaranteed so many debts that there is still no assurance of repayment. An alternative is for another corporation to guarantee payment, which works if the customer is a subsidiary of another entity whose financial condition is strong. If the customer or its guarantor signs a guarantee agreement, be sure to attach it to a UCC-1 form and file the completed documents in the jurisdiction where the goods reside. This gives the company added protection in case the customer has issued numerous guarantees, putting the company in a senior position to all other claims for which a UCC-1 form was not filed prior to the company's filing date.

An alternative to a guarantee is to obtain credit insurance. Under this approach, an insurance company evaluates the company's customers and allows the company to grant a maximum amount of credit to each one. The insurance company will guarantee payment up to the amount of credit it has authorized. The company can pass the credit insurance cost to its customers, who are frequently willing to do so in exchange for having a credit line with the company. Also, if the company wishes to shoulder some credit risk, it can issue a larger line of credit and rely on the insurance company's guarantee only for the lower credit level. A side benefit of this arrangement is that the company's accounts receivable are perceived by lenders to be of a higher quality (since bad debt risks are eliminated), so more receivables can be used as collateral for a line of credit.

If the company is selling higher-cost fixed assets, it should consider aligning itself with a leasing agency. By doing so, it can offer leasing terms to its customers. Under this approach, the leasing agency takes on the risk of collection, while the company obtains immediate payment in full from the leasing agency as soon as it delivers the goods to the customer. Further, the leasing agency may pay the company a small percentage of the interest earned on the lease in exchange for referring customer business to it. Alternatively, the company can take on the leasing program itself, though this means that it is accepting a considerable amount of credit risk that can result in substantial losses. If a company chooses this path, it will need to set aside significant reserves for bad debt losses and also charge a sufficiently high interest rate not only to cover potential losses but also to earn a profit by engaging in the leasing business.

It may also be possible to issue goods to customers under a consignment arrangement. Under this approach, the company continues to own any goods shipped until such time as the customer sells them to a third party. At that point, the customer remits payment for the sold items to the company. This approach requires a great deal of attention to inventory tracking at potentially a multitude of customer locations, and so requires a significant amount of staff time to manage. Also, one must enter into a consignment agreement with each customer, outlining the level of insurance coverage the customer must maintain over the goods, the number of days the customer has in which to pay the company once a sale is made, how the company can reclaim its goods, and so on. Further, the company must file a UCC-1 financing statement in the jurisdiction where the customer is located and notify all lien holders that the financing statement has been filed. Otherwise, if the customer were to enter bankruptcy, the company would have no legal right to the return of its goods.

Even without a formal consignment agreement, a company can obtain a similar lien position on goods sent to a customer by obtaining a purchase money security interest (PMSI). To do this, the customer must sign a PMSI statement, after which the company must send the notice to all other lien holders who have filed a UCC-1 security interest in the customer's assets. Then the company files a UCC-1 and the PMSI in the Secretary of State's office where the customer's primary place of business is located. By going through these steps, the company has a right to the return of its own goods or payment for them from the customer, in advance of the claims of all other lien holders.

If the credit staff will grant credit only in exchange for a lien on customer goods or property, it may run into trouble if a more senior lien already exists. This is typically the case when a bank has issued a loan to the customer in exchange for a blanket lien on all of its assets. If the company sells goods that the customer must have, there may be enough leverage to demand that a senior lien holder subordinate its claim to customer assets, placing the company's claim in a senior position. Such an agreement requires the completion of a subordination document, which is usually so specific to a particular situation that legal counsel should review each one in detail. Given a senior lien holder's unwillingness to relinquish its claim position, this option is not commonly used.

If there seems to be reasonable grounds to grant credit, but the amount to be granted is less than what the customer requests, consider combining shortened terms with a reduced credit limit. For example, if a customer requests a $10,000 credit line with a payment interval of 30 days, the credit department can instead grant a $5,000 line with a 15-day payment interval. By doing so, the customer can still effectively use $10,000 of credit by placing orders for $5,000 every 15 days. This approach works only if the customer has a sufficiently rapid cash flow cycle to pay on such short terms, and if its orders can be split into these smaller sizes.

If an international customer is applying for credit, consider requiring a letter of credit (LOC). Under this payment mechanism, the customer applies to its bank for an LOC, which examines the creditworthiness of the customer and (if acceptable) promises to pay the company on behalf of the customer when all terms of the business transaction have been completed. An LOC is time-consuming to arrange and requires exact adherence to the terms of the LOC before the bank will issue payment. Given these difficulties, an alternative is to obtain an export credit guarantee from the Export-Import Bank (www.exim.gov). The bank will require a substantial amount of financial information about the customer, increasing in amount with the size of the prospective delivery, and will charge a fee to issue a guarantee. However, it will guarantee only a portion of the delivery, so the company will still have credit risk for some of the accounts receivable. Also, the bank considers some countries to be too risky, and will not guarantee any shipments to those locations, irrespective of the financial condition of the customer.

If a salesperson is exceptionally pushy in trying to have the credit department grant unrestricted credit to a customer, the credit manager can consider striking a deal with the salesperson—if there is any collection difficulty, the salesperson will be primarily responsible for collecting the funds. By putting this in writing and sending a copy to the salesperson, the credit department is making it very clear that the salesperson will share in the collection task, which may give him pause in his quest to have a large credit line approved.

(c) PERIODICALLY REVIEWING CREDIT LIMITS. The initial granting of a line of credit matches the financial condition of a customer only at the time of the initial credit application. Over time, it is likely that a revised level of credit will be necessary. However, given the large number of customers to whom most companies have granted credit, it can be difficult for the credit department to regularly review all customers to determine the most appropriate level of credit.

One way to handle the problem is to review the credit levels of only the top 20 percent of customers each year, measured by sales volume. The logic behind this approach is that sales to this group of customers generally make up 80 percent of all sales, so ensuring that credit levels are correct for this group will shield the company from any significant levels of credit risk. Thus, if a company doing a smaller amount of business with the company goes bankrupt, the amount of its bad debt will be so small that the company will not be adversely impacted to any significant degree.

There are other ways to select customers whose credit levels may require a review. For example, if a customer pays with a check that is returned due to nonsufficient funds, this is a clear sign that its financial condition is declining. Though the occurrence of just one NSF check may be due to a miscalculation by the accounts payable staff regarding its bank balance, a repetition of this event certainly calls for an immediate credit review. Another approach is to watch for customers who pay some invoices but not all (known as *invoice skipping*). For example, when a customer has several invoices to pay the company, it pays only a few of the smaller ones and delays payment on the largest invoices until chided by the collection staff. When detected, this should also result in a credit review. A third condition is when customers stop taking cash discounts. Though this could be the result of a new accounts payable person paying a customer's bills, if cash discounts continue to not be paid after a reminder notice, it is likely that the customer's finances have taken a downturn. The presence of NSF checks, invoice skipping, and missed cash discounts can all be readily detected, but usually by other parts of the accounting department, not the credit department. Thus, some coordination among different departments is needed to ensure that credit reviews are conducted based on these warning flags.

(d) INVOICE CREATION. One of the biggest problems with late customer payments is the invoices sent to customers. This section contains a number of recommendations for improving invoices.

Invoicing problems begin in the billing department with improper training. Junior staff people with minimal experience frequently enter the accounting department through this functional area, so there is a high risk that invoices will not contain correct information or will be sent to the wrong location. To keep this from happening, run every new employee through a closely supervised training program and follow up at intervals to ensure that they are adhering to the prescribed invoicing regimen. There should be a billing procedure to supplement the training program and that is readily available for review if the staff has a billing question.

If a customer detects a problem on an invoice, the invoice usually lists no contact information at all. As a result, the customer may set the invoice to one side and wait for a collections person to call, rather than attempting to wade through the company's phone system to reach the correct person. Since this behavior will result in late payments, it is better to list a contact phone number on each invoice in a highlighted area. Further, if the company accepts credit card payments, the contact phone number for this person should also be listed on the invoice, thereby facilitating more rapid payment.

Another problem with the invoice is that customers usually have to calculate the due date, since the invoice does not give them this information. Instead, it lists an invoice date and payment terms. Customers usually enter today's date into their accounts payable system rather than the due date, and also use the default payment terms, which may not match the terms listed on the invoice. By simply presenting them with the date on which it is due, there is much less room for customer error.

The same approach should be used with early payment discounts. Rather than listing the invoice creation date and discount terms, just state the amount to pay by an early date, and a larger amount to pay by a later date. For example, an invoice could read "Amount due if paid by May 15: $119.20" and then on the next line, "Amount due if paid by June 1: $125.00."

An additional problem is the amount of information listed on an invoice. Some companies have listed far too much, such as the customer number, quote number, and internal order number, not to mention the name of the salesperson, sales region, and discount terms so compressed that they look like early Egyptian. Given so much data to wade through, customers may enter the wrong information in their accounts payable systems, resulting in payment problems. The most common problem of all is that they cannot determine the invoice number, and so enter some other number into their systems, which then appears on the remittance advice accompanying any check payments, giving the cash application staff considerable trouble trying to figure out what the customers are paying. To avoid this problem, simplify the invoice layout to the greatest extent possible, leaving only the information most needed by customers.

Customers have an annoying habit of changing their addresses from time to time, which can result in invoices being delayed in the postal system. In order to be kept current on customer address changes, stamp the words *Address Correction Requested* on each envelope. Then, if a customer leaves a forwarding address, the Postal Service will notify the company. Of course, this also calls for a procedure whereby the mailroom staff knows that these notices are to be forwarded to the billing department, where they can be used to update the billing database.

Another way to obtain updated customer address information is from the sales staff. They usually keep and update a list of contact addresses separate from the one used by the accounting department. If the billing staff has recurring invoices of a sufficiently large size to make this approach worth the sales staff's time, send a list of prospective billings to them and ask for any contact updates. The sales staff will be most obliging if they have a commission riding on a timely customer payment.

Recurring invoices present an opportunity for early payment. Since the billing staff usually has a good idea of the exact amount of these invoices well before the beginning of the month (when they are normally issued), consider shifting the accounting system into the next accounting period, running these invoices several days early but with the first day of the next month listed as the invoice date, and issuing them in advance to customers. By doing so, customers have more time to process the invoices through their payables systems, resulting in earlier payments to the company.

Some customers have a complex internal processing system wherein they will not pay an invoice unless they have matched it to a document showing proof of receipt. This can delay payment a great deal, especially if they never locate the proof of receipt and instead just wait for the company to call them about a late payment and then thrust the proof of receipt problem on it. To avoid this problem, consider shipping using an overnight delivery service that posts a receipt signature on its web site. Then delay invoicing until the shipment has been received, access the web site to obtain an image of the receipt information with a signature image, and cut and paste this extra information directly into the invoice.

When invoices are complex, there is a high degree of risk that some billing information will be inaccurate. This may involve incorrect pricing discounts, marketing rebates, or other variations on the standard price list. Whatever the reason, this type of invoice is much more highly debated by customers, resulting in significantly slower payment intervals. To keep this from happening, have someone other than the invoice preparer proofread all complex invoices before they go to customers. Even if invoices are relatively simple, the risk of having a large payment delayed due to an inaccuracy is too great, so have larger invoices of all types proofread.

An even better approach is to use no invoicing at all. Instead, have customers fill out an ACH authorization form, listing their bank account information. The company can then deduct the amounts due directly from their bank accounts. This approach works best for small-dollar, highly repetitive payments wherein the payment processing cost is a large proportion of the total amount due. Customers with large balances want more control over their payments and will not usually agree to this approach.

There are also filing inefficiencies associated with invoicing. The main problem is the separate filing of multiple invoice copies. One may be filed alphabetically, another by invoice number, and a third sent to another department (such as customer service) to be filed in yet another location. Not only does this require a large amount of filing labor, but there is a heightened risk that one or more copies will be filed in the wrong place, requiring a large amount of time to locate. Consequently, it is better to print just two copies—one for the customer and one to be filed internally—and eliminate all other copies. This has the side benefit of reducing the cost of invoices, which are no longer needed in anything larger than a two-part form.

Finally, consider not issuing a monthly statement of account to customers. It involves a mailing to every customer with an overdue balance, which may represent many statements. Also, the payable staffs who receive the statements do not have time to research one that may include any number of errors caused by the company's cash application staff, as well as multiple unresolved deductions. Consequently, they usually throw away statements without reading them. Given their low success rate, issuing statements is not an efficient use of the billing staff's time.

(e) INVOICE DELIVERY. There are a variety of ways to deliver invoices that will enhance the speed of collection. Not all the options noted in this section will work for every company, and may even be worse than whatever approach is currently being used, so be sure to review the merits of each one before attempting an installation.

The prime issue involving invoice delivery is simply to print them every day. If a billing clerk prefers to let billing information accumulate until there is a large batch to process, the company is unintentionally delaying its prospective receipt of cash. Thus, the controller should periodically compare the shipping log to the invoice register to ensure that invoices are being issued in a timely manner.

Some customers process payments only on specific days of the week or month. If an invoice arrives after a check-printing date, it must wait for the next regularly scheduled payment date. Also, some customers require the accumulation of several pieces of information before they authorize payment. Whatever those requirements may be, the billing staff is obligated to ensure that they are met, not to mention issuing invoices so that they arrive well before the next customer payment date. If a customer is especially picky about its payment authorization procedures, consider contacting them, documenting all their requirements, and integrating these additional tasks into the billing process.

When a company has large and complex invoices involving multiple, large-dollar line items, there is an increased chance that customers will find something on their invoices to debate, which delays payment of the entire invoice. Though one can encourage them to at least pay the undisputed part of the invoice right away, an alternative is to issue a separate invoice for each line item of significant dollar size. When mailed as a single packet, customers can quickly sort through them, extract those under debate, and submit the remainder for payment.

The opposite approach may work better if there are many shipments of very small dollar amounts through each month. If so, the invoicing cost may be a large proportion of the total cost of each shipment. To reduce this cost, one can wait until month-end and issue a single summarized invoice. This approach interferes with cash flow to some extent, and so must be limited to low-dollar shipments.

When a company uses its own staff to deliver goods to customers, the accounting staff can give them an invoice when they leave the company location. They can then deliver the invoice along with the delivery, thereby eliminating the mailing interval. However, customers don't normally have a procedure for the handling of invoices left at the receiving dock, so invoices can be lost within the customer location. Thus, it is better for the delivery staff to walk the invoice directly to the customer's accounting department or at least its mailroom, which is more accustomed to handling such documents.

When a delivery is made, customers may review the goods at the receiving dock and reject some items, making an invoice inaccurate before it even reaches the customer. To avoid this problem, consider having the delivery person create an invoice on the spot, either manually or with a portable computer, using updated delivery quantities. By doing so, there will be no deduction problems that could otherwise interfere with timely invoice payments.

An excellent approach for delivering invoices is to purchase a copy of Adobe Acrobat and install it in the computer containing the corporate accounting system. Once installed, a new printer will appear on the computer, called "Distiller." Select this printing option, and a portable document format (PDF) invoice will be stored in the computer. One can then e-mail this PDF invoice directly to customers, who need only the free Acrobat Reader software to access it. Not only does this approach eliminate the mailing delay, but it also allows the receiving company to pass the invoice through its internal e-mail system for approvals, thereby speeding up the payment process even further.

(f) CASH COLLECTION AND APPLICATION. The cash application process begins not when a company receives a customer payment, but actually when the customer cuts the check. If the company can eliminate the mail float from the customer, it can obtain use of the cash several days sooner, while also striking the payment from its accounts receivable listing, which gives the collection staff fewer late invoices to pursue. One way to obtain checks sooner is to send the sales staff to pick them up. This works best if they are already planning a visit and can drop by the accounts payable department without going too far out of their way. This is an improved approach even if the sales staff then has to mail the check to the company, since this at least verifies that the check has indeed been mailed.

If there is no sales staff available, consider hiring a local messenger service to pick up the check and mail it to the company. Since this is expensive, use it only when the collection staff has a great deal of trouble getting a customer to pay. It is a more broadly applicable solution than using one's sales staff, since messenger services are available in all major cities.

Another way to shorten the mailing interval is to have customers send payments to a lockbox. Lockboxes are operated by local banks, and can be positioned in multiple locations throughout the country. Each customer is asked to send its payments to the lockbox nearest to it, thereby shortening the mailing interval to as little as one day. Larger banks are now posting the images of received checks on the Internet, so the cash application staff can access this information quickly and update the accounts receivable records. Since a company's customer base will change over time, this necessitates an occasional review of lockbox locations to ensure that they are arranged properly to ensure the minimum amount of mailing delay.

An alternative to the lockbox concept is to issue the corporate account number for an overnight delivery service to selected customers. By doing so, a company can more readily convince customers to send in payments on a rush basis. Given the cost of overnight delivery services, this approach is cost-effective only for larger payments.

It may be possible to entirely avoid payments with cash. Instead, consider accepting credit card payments over the phone. To make this option as broadly applicable as possible, accept all major credit cards. It may also be possible to offer a small cash discount in exchange for paying by credit card, though when combined with the transaction fees charged by credit card processors, the result may be a significant reduction in one's margins.

A key area in which the application of cash to open accounts receivable impacts the collection function is clearing up any unapplied payments. When the cash application staff runs across these items, they tend to shunt them off to one side and address them only during their spare time. The trouble is that these payments represent items most likely to involve the collection staff, with various deductions removed from them. By giving their resolution a higher priority, one can reduce the subsequent workload of the collection department.

Another cash application task impacting collectors is the handling of restrictive endorsements on checks. If cashed, a check on which the words *Final Payment* are written can make it extremely difficult for one to collect any remaining outstanding funds on an account receivable. Consequently, the cash application staff must be aware of the legal impact of restrictive endorsements, and immediately forward these checks to a legal expert for further review before cashing them.

(g) MANAGING THE COLLECTION DEPARTMENT. The collection department is responsible for converting a large amount of receivables into cash as soon as possible, which greatly impacts a company's financial health. Setting up the department to operate in the most efficient manner possible greatly contributes to this goal. This section offers a number of possibilities for enhanced management of the department.

The collection department suffers from a great deal of compartmentalization. It relies on customer order information from the order entry department, while the credit department can make loose credit decisions that give the collections staff fits. An alternative is to consider combining all three departments, both physically and under one manager. By doing so, the group can operate under the same goals and more easily share information. Under this arrangement, it is more likely that the combined department will also use fully integrated computer systems.

It is also useful to hire a collection manager with substantial training and experience in the field. Too many collection functions rely upon "homegrown" staff who have no idea of how to run the department in an efficient manner. By bringing in an expert, one can rely upon this person to properly organize the department, train the staff, and ensure that customers are contacted promptly and effectively.

As was the case for a collection manager, be sure to assign staff to the collection role on a full-time basis. Because many people consider the collection task to be distasteful, they tend to put it off while they complete other work first, which leads to spotty collection results. Instead, create a position for formal collectors who do nothing but collections, and whose performance is based solely on collection results.

Collectors tend to fall into a rut when it comes to collection techniques, and also may not have the best collection manners when talking to customers. By sending them to formal collection training programs, one can greatly improve their collection technique, while also giving them a variety of collection tools from which to choose. Training classes are widely available, as are books on the subject. The National Association of Credit Managers (www.nacm.com) offers a great deal of training information.

Collection responsibility for a specific customer may not be clearly defined, so there is confusion between the sales and collection staffs regarding who is contacting the customer next. This inevitably introduces a great deal of delay to the collection of cash. To avoid this, place primary collection responsibility for each customer on specific collectors, so all correspondence runs through them. If the sales staff is asked to assist in a collection effort, the designated collector still monitors and records all activities. This gives customers little "wiggle room" to play off different collectors and salespeople against each other.

It may be useful to periodically shift collection responsibilities among the collection staff, so that different people are contacting different customers. By doing so, customers are exposed to different collection techniques that may jar loose payments somewhat sooner than would otherwise be the case. Also, collectors can form close ties to customers, resulting in their empathizing with the customers to such a degree that they are more lenient in allowing time to pay. Shifting collectors to new customers can break these ties, resulting in better collection performance.

On top of controlling collection responsibilities, one should also build the collection staff's workday around prime calling hours, which are usually in the morning in customers' time zones. This may call for unusually early or late working hours for the staff, depending on where they are calling, and may also require the scheduling of all other activities around these hours, so customer contacts can be made without any interruption.

In any given time period, there may be a great many overdue invoices to collect and only a few collectors to follow up on problem accounts. If so, be sure to formally stratify the invoices, assigning top collection priority to the largest-dollar items. By doing so, collectors stay focused on the main goal of the department—bringing in the largest dollar volume of cash. Though this approach may result in some smaller invoices eventually becoming bad debts, this is better than having a large invoice not be collected!

An alternative to invoice stratification is to assign the best collectors to the worst customers. Some collectors have a superb ability to extract payment, so put them on the most difficult accounts (which may not be the largest ones) and shift more junior or less talented staff to easier accounts. An alternative is to use only new staff to make initial customer contacts prior to invoice due dates to see if there are any upcoming problems, and use senior collectors to make all collection calls subsequent to the invoice date. This approach allows new collectors to initially make low-pressure calls while they are still learning their jobs and build up customer contacts in a more relaxed environment.

Despite the best allocation of work among collectors, some invoices will never be collected. Rather than subjecting collectors to the paperwork needed to document every bad debt and obtain approval from a manager, just allow them to write off smaller balances with no extra approval. This approach wastes less of their time, giving them more time to make additional collection calls.

Maintaining a high level of communication with both the sales department and customers is a high priority for collectors, since it results in a higher level of collection success. For example, meet with the sales department on a regular basis in order to discuss collection policies and procedures with them, and to hear their concerns. Also, go on sales calls with the sales staff in order to meet with customers, or go alone to meet with one's accounts payable counterparts at larger customers. By creating these key relationships, it is much easier to obtain payment from customers, while also forming stronger bonds with the sales department, which may then be more inclined to assist with collection efforts.

In the spirit of having strong relations with the sales staff, consider e-mailing them the accounts receivable aging report. This is easy with most accounting systems, which allows one to export the aging to an Excel spreadsheet, which can then be sorted by salesperson and added to an e-mail as an attachment. If there are many accounts, consider e-mailing only the overdue invoices from the aging report, thereby focusing the sales staff's attention on the most important collection problems.

A management issue that involves the sales department but impacts the collections department is the structure of the corporate commission plan. If the sales staff is paid a commission only when customers have paid the company, they will be much more likely to assist in the collection effort. Further, if they receive no commission at all if a payment is more than 90 days late (or some such figure), then they will be particularly aggressive in collecting payment. At a minimum, recommend revoking commissions for all bad debts incurred, so a salesperson will eventually see a subtraction from his commission statement for invoices that have been written off.

An excellent way to analyze the reasons why bad debts occurred is to schedule meetings with all relevant departments to conduct postmortems on bad debts. The purpose of these meetings is not to point fingers, but rather to ascertain why bad debts occurred and what can be done to prevent the situation from arising in the future. These meetings are most effective if specific responsibility is given for fixing internal problems and if senior management enforces the resolution of these issues.

Performance feedback can have a powerful positive effect on a company's collection effort. For example, consider posting collection results for each collector in a public place, and pay small bonuses for outstanding performance. Also consider awarding small bonuses to the sales staff if they have assisted to an unusual extent with collection efforts. This concept can also be used in a negative manner by reporting on which salespeople's accounts result in the largest dollar volume of bad debts, though this approach should be used with a considerable amount of care in order to avoid worsening relations with the sales department.

27.2A COLLECTION POLICIES, PROCEDURES, AND SYSTEMS (NEW)

A collection department must deal with a multitude of tasks every day, so many that it is easy for the department to gradually become disorganized as various employees create their own collection systems, use different approaches for dealing with customers, and generally present an inconsistent corporate "face" to customers. In this section, we discuss the use of policies, procedures, and systems to yield a sufficient level of organization to keep these problems from ever happening.

The collection department requires a policies-and-procedures manual. This document describes how employees deal with specific collection problems, when various collection techniques can be used, what authorizations are required for various actions, and when accounts should be handed to a collection agency or law firm. Further, it should specify when the collection staff should communicate various problems to other parts of the company, such as the initiation of credit-hold status or a sudden increase in bad debts that may require a change in the credit-granting policy. Though valuable, this document does little good if one does not indoctrinate the collection staff in its use.

One can disseminate the collection manual somewhat more widely by showing it to the sales staff, who is directly impacted by it. This can involve presentations at periodic sales meetings, or even formal training sessions for new sales staff. By taking these steps, the sales staff will have a better understanding of when collectors are about to take a serious collections action, which is useful for dealing with customers. However, if the collection manager chooses to alter the manual, be sure to notify the sales staff, who will otherwise assume that the old version is still governing the actions of the collection staff.

An extremely important system for organizing the collection department is the use of a collection database. At a minimum, this should include a listing of who last contacted a customer, what was said, and when payment was promised. For a single collection person, this can be a few notes jotted down on the last accounts receivable aging report. However, a more complex system is needed if many collectors are involved. At its most technically advanced, a collection database is fully computerized, with an interface to the accounting system so it can access the latest overdue account information. It may also plan collector calls to match customer time zones, allow for automated document faxes to customers, and be linked to a document management system so that electronic versions of billing-related documents can be accessed without leaving one's chair. Though expensive, these systems can result in massive efficiency improvements in larger collection departments.

It may be useful to maintain additional customer files. For example, one can maintain a list of alternative customer contacts, such as the accounts payable manager, assistant controller, controller, chief financial officer, and president, all with associated phone, fax, and e-mail information. If used sparingly, one can occasionally tap these other people with some success to assist in particularly difficult collection problems. It is easiest to collect this information by asking for it when each customer fills out a credit application form. Another useful file is a list of personal information about customer contacts, such as their birthdays, names of children, and other information that may surprise and please customers if brought up from time to time. By doing so, customers begin to feel that collectors are taking a personal interest in them, which makes them easier to deal with over collection issues.

The collection staff should also have access to the customer orders database. This is the listing of orders submitted by customers but not yet filled by the company. Knowing that a particularly large order is about to ship can be an excellent point of leverage in order to obtain payment for a past-due invoice if the alternative is a held shipment. Access to this information can be difficult if a company has not installed an integrated set of computer systems that cross departmental boundaries.

An important policy is the uniform administration of late fees. The Robinson-Patman Act does not allow price discrimination among a company's customers who are of the same class. Thus, forcing one customer to pay a late fee and not another can be a violation of this federal statute. Consequently, there should be a policy and related procedure in place defining exactly when late fees are to be charged and when they can be waived. Also, be sure to regularly educate the collection staff regarding this issue, so there is no inadvertent breaking of the law.

Some customers need only a reminder prior to a scheduled payment date to make a payment. To ensure that customers have all the necessary information to authorize a payment, a company can install an automated fax system that assembles electronic images of the invoice, related purchase order, and bill of lading, and fax this information to all customers in one nightly batch. Although it is an expensive system to install, one can reap substantial benefits from it, not only through faster customer payments but also by eliminating the same work that the collections staff would otherwise have to do.

The same approach can be used to issue dunning letters automatically. The computer system automatically issues a boilerplate dunning letter, modified to include customer-specific contact and invoice information, by fax to all customers whose payments have not arrived as of their due dates. Once again, this can be an expensive system to install, so it is cost-justified only if there are a great many dunning letters to send.

Some customers normally pay slowly if not badgered by a collection staff. After a few billing cycles, it becomes quite obvious which customers fall into this category. The collection manager should have a system for monitoring repeatedly late-paying customers and flagging them in the accounting system for early contact by the collection staff. By doing so, there is a regimented system in place for going after repeat offenders as soon as possible.

The same approach can be used for any large invoice, simply on the grounds that late payment for anything involving large dollars is worth additional up-front effort to ensure timely payment. This can involve a procedure for sending reminder letters, with attached invoices, to all customers whose latest billings exceed a preset dollar value. One should note the early-reminder notice date on the department calendar, so it is regularly followed.

It is useful to institute a standard procedure for periodically altering the mode of communication with customers. By doing so, the collection staff is more likely to find the correct person at a customer location who can approve an invoice payment. For example, one can begin by sending an invoice copy by e-mail, following it up with a fax, then a phone call, and finally via an overnight delivery service. If a company is unable to route an invoice to the recipient through one of these avenues, it probably does not deserve to be in business!

The same approach of systematically altering communications can also be applied to dunning letters. One can schedule ongoing alterations to both the content and issuance timing of dunning letters, thereby throwing off any customers who are timing their payments to coincide with the usual round of letters leading up to but never quite reaching legal action. By constantly changing the pattern of these letters, customers are more likely to pay sooner.

(a) COLLECTION TECHNIQUES. There are many techniques used to collect funds from customers. This section covers a wide range of them, beginning with more preventive and friendly methods, and progressing to more aggressive and confrontational ones.

The best preventive collection technique of all is to call customers and thank them for making payments on time. This positive behavior startles customers so much that they go out of their way to make timely payments in the future. It also initiates a pleasant relationship that the collection staff may find useful if it must call about late payments at some point in the future. Calling to thank customers can be time-consuming, so don't practice it all the time—just enough to create a good impression with the larger customers.

Another preventive approach is to have customers sign an electronic funds transfer document in advance, usually as part of the credit application form. By doing so, one can be assured of immediate payment on the invoice due date. However, most customers are uncomfortable with this approach, so it tends to be enforceable only for frequently recurring billing situations for an amount unlikely to be disputed, such as a monthly parking bill.

An easy preventive collection technique is to determine which customers post upcoming payment information on their web sites for suppliers to access. Obtain access codes for these sites and regularly compare posted payment dates to the company's accounts receivable aging to see if any invoices are not appearing on the customer's site or vary in amount. By doing so, one can contact customers immediately, usually well before the payment due date, to determine what is wrong and to resolve the issue as rapidly as possible.

Another preventive collection technique is to keep track of collection problems caused by special pricing situations such as volume discounts, and continuously bring these issues to the attention of the sales manager, accompanied by a request to simplify the pricing structure sufficiently to avoid having it cause collection problems. This is not normally worth pursuing unless there is a large volume of collection activity centered around pricing issues, because battling the sales department over pricing policy can be difficult.

Once the payment due date passes with no payment in hand, it is best to eliminate any grace period and immediately begin calling customers. By doing so, cash receipts are accelerated, while customers receive a clear message that the company takes its payment terms seriously. This approach is problematic only if the collection staff is already so overwhelmed with collection problems that it has no time to make additional calls to customers who may already have a check in the mail.

Once a payment is clearly past due, many collection departments prefer to first send a low-key reminder letter, while their staffs personally call about older invoices that have obvious problems. This is not the best approach, since some recently overdue invoices may be so large that letting them drag a few additional days will greatly impact corporate cash flow. It is therefore better to use dunning letters only for smaller overdue balances and call at once for larger items. Also consider sending dunning letters by e-mail rather than the Postal Service in order to eliminate the mail float. Further, consider sending dunning letters to people outside the usual payment process, such as the controller or chief financial officer. These people are not used to receiving dunning letters and probably don't want to again, so they will use their authority to ensure more rapid payment.

An alternative to the dunning letter is the attorney letter. Some attorneys charge only a modest fee for sending a boilerplate collection letter on their letterhead. This type of notice may scare a customer into thinking that a lawsuit is just around the corner, resulting in more rapid payment.

A very low-key variation on the dunning and attorney letters is to copy the overdue invoice, stamp *Overdue* on it in some glaringly colorful ink, and send this to the customer. The stamp will gain the recipient's attention, and possibly spur action if the invoice really has been lost somewhere in the customer's payables system.

If customers have an ongoing habit of losing invoices, be sure to send a replacement either by certified mail or via an overnight delivery service that requires a receipt signature. If lost yet again, one can then present the customer with the receiving documentation. This approach can also be used for the initial delivery of an invoice, though its expense calls for prudent application.

Another ploy customers use is the classic "it's in the mail" approach when they have not even cut the check. Though one can ask for the check number and date in order to gain some comfort regarding the check's existence, a glib payables person can make up this information on the spot. If a customer uses this approach multiple times, consider playing hardball and having the customer cancel the check (if it ever existed) and send a wire transfer instead. One can even offer to pay for the wire transfer and check cancellation charge in order to overcome any remaining customer objections. However, if this approach is used, agree to pay these charges only after seeing some evidence, such as the customer's bank statement. Otherwise, the company may be paying for expenses that the customer never incurred.

If a customer is debating just a portion of an invoice, it tends to avoid paying the entire amount until the debated issued has been resolved. When this occurs, push for immediate payment of whatever portion of the invoice is not in dispute. This can be difficult, since some customers like to use the remaining invoice balance as leverage in obtaining agreement to its demands on the disputed item.

If a customer makes a payment commitment, be sure to write down this information and send a confirming letter to the customer. If there are a series of payments to be made, note the amount and due date of each one in the letter. This approach formalizes the payment arrangement while also letting the customer know that the collection staff will be closely monitoring payment timeliness.

If a customer claims not to have sufficient funds to pay off an account receivable right away, try having him sign a promissory note. Not only does this tie the customer into a fixed payment schedule, but it is also much easier to collect in court, since the customer has clearly stated his obligation to pay a debt. If this approach works, consider leaving the related invoice on the accounts receivable aging report rather than recording it as a note receivable, so the collection staff will constantly see the outstanding balance and be reminded to check on the timeliness of subsequent payments against the note.

If there is no way to obtain any kind of payment in the near term, see if the customer will ship back any goods it may still have in stock, even if this is only a small portion of the original shipment. By doing so, the company retains the option to resell the goods elsewhere. This approach must be taken as early as possible, before the goods vanish from the customer site, and may also require a markdown on resale if the goods show any sign of having been used.

An alternative to a merchandise return is having the customer pay in kind, which may involve any type of goods or service that the customer sells. This approach works only if the company actually needs the "in kind" payment, and if the collection staff thinks the customer will be in business long enough to fulfill its obligation to the company.

There are a small number of situations in which a company and its customer sell to each other, so each one has outstanding accounts receivable due to the other. If the customer is late in making a payment, it is possible in these situations to offset one's obligation to the customer with the customer's overdue account receivable. However, this can cause a great deal of payment confusion between the accounting departments of the two companies, so be sure to document exactly which invoices are being offset and send this letter to the customer's controller.

If there is no way to obtain payment through any normal collection approach, consider filling out a small claims court complaint form and sending it to the customer. While not actually filing the claim, this tells the customer that the company is serious about collection and intends to take the matter to court if no resolution can be reached before that time. If this does not work, then file the claim and pursue the matter in small claims court. This approach works only if the unpaid amount is less than the maximum set by the small claims court in whose jurisdiction the matter falls. If the unpaid amount is only slightly higher than the maximum, consider forgoing the excess and filing a claim for the maximum allowable amount instead.

Filing in a regular court is certainly an option if the unpaid amount is too high to fall under the jurisdiction of a small claims court. However, lawsuits are extremely expensive and time-consuming, and may cost more than the amount of any eventual settlement. Consequently, it is prudent to first investigate the customer to verify that it has sufficient assets to be able to pay any forthcoming judgment. If not, write off the unpaid amount as a bad debt.

If a lawsuit has resulted in a judgment in the company's favor, it may still be extremely difficult to obtain payment. To do so, retain the services of a lawyer who has experience in collecting money judgments. Even if these lawyers charge extra for their services, they are well worth it.

An unusual role for the collection department is disposing of credit balances. These usually arise when customers double-pay an invoice or are granted a deduction credit but pay the full invoice amount instead. Whatever the reason, these credits are subject to unclaimed property laws, which require that they eventually be paid to the local state government. Rather than have this happen, consider contacting customers to see if they want to apply the credits to additional orders (which increases sales) or just want the money returned. In either case, this increases customer goodwill, and is well worth the effort.

No matter which of the preceding collection methods are used, remember that entering into a discussion with a customer requires an open mind regarding how to obtain payment. This should not involve a bombastic approach resulting in poor relations; on the contrary, listen hard to what the customer is saying, and craft a solution that will work for both parties. This may call for negotiation of a payment option that is less than the company would like but that still ensures eventual payment of the open balance, which is the goal of the collection department.

(b) DEDUCTION MANAGEMENT. In some industries, vast amounts of deductions are so common that it is unusual to receive a customer payment that does not include a deduction for one reason or another. This is especially common in the retail sector. The collection staff can be buried under a virtual avalanche of deductions, so it is critical to set up a formal process for dealing with them, as noted in this section.

The first step in managing deductions is to create a standard procedure for it and to train the collection staff in its use. This procedure should itemize exactly how deductions of different sizes are to be handled, such as through an immediate write-off, calls to customers, in-person meetings, bill-backs, or the complete termination of all credit. It is also helpful to send a "how to" deductions instruction sheet to customers, detailing how they can take deductions, authorizations required, and what related paperwork to send to the company. This high level of formalization eliminates some deductions entirely and gives the collection staff a structure with which to deal with the remainder.

Central to the process of formalizing the deduction process is just that—centralization. It is extremely difficult to efficiently process deductions when they are routed through a large number of people, any one of whom can delay the resolution process ad infinitum. Instead, use the concept of process centering to assign each deduction to one person. That person is responsible for all aspects of the deduction resolution, including following up with other people within the company to obtain additional information relevant to the resolution process. This approach greatly reduces the total time required to eliminate deductions from the accounting records.

It is possible to detect deductions before they occur, especially in the area of product pricing. When an invoice contains prices obviously different from the prices listed in a customer's purchase order, it is entirely likely that the customer will pay based on the lower of the two, which may not be the invoice price. To avoid this problem, conduct either a manual or an automated comparison of the invoice and purchase order before mailing the invoice, and resolve any pricing discrepancies on the spot.

Another major source of deductions is trade promotion information, such as a percentage discount if a customer places an order by a certain date. The marketing department needs to send this information to the billing department before or no later than when it goes to customers, so the accountants can factor it into their invoiced prices. Otherwise, the collection staff must waste time researching these deductions at a later date.

When first cleaning up a large volume of deductions, there may be so many to resolve that the collection staff is buried from the start. If so, consider prioritizing deduction resolution by declining dollar volume. By doing so, one can reduce the total dollars of deductions on the books, thereby improving the quality of the total accounts receivable balance. Also, this approach allows one to determine the underlying reasons for the most important deduction problems and to eliminate them, thereby keeping larger deductions from occurring in the future.

The only way to truly eliminate the bulk of deduction issues is to focus on their underlying causes. To do so, create a database in which the collection staff notes the reason for each deduction; then summarize this information on a regular basis and present it to management for resolution. For larger companies, this can require an elaborate database and workflow tracking system, though smaller organizations can easily monitor this information with an electronic spreadsheet.

Many deductions are extremely small and are not worth the time of the collection staff to research and settle with customers. In these cases, consider giving the accounting or customer service departments the authority to immediately approve small deductions. However, it is still useful to track them at a summary level in order to see if some customers are abusing their deduction privileges by taking large quantities of small deductions.

Customers sometimes take payment deductions due to goods being damaged in transit. A company guards against this problem by obtaining shipping insurance and charging the added cost to the customer. However, some cost-conscious customers do not want to incur this added charge, leaving the company with the difficult decision of absorbing shipping insurance or accepting damaged goods deductions. The solution is to send a letter to each customer who refuses to pay for shipping insurance, asking for their formal signed authorization to ship goods to them without insurance. By keeping this signed document as proof when the next customer deduction occurs, the collection staff is in a much stronger bargaining position when it attempts to obtain payment.

When a customer takes an extremely large deduction, there is obviously a significant problem occurring that may interfere with the overall business relationship. In these cases, it may make sense to visit the customer in person to discuss the problem. By doing so, one can get to the root of the problem more quickly, while also building a much higher level of communication with the customer than would otherwise be the case. This is also a good time to learn of any special shipping or billing requirements imposed by the customer that may be interfering with timely payment.

Sometimes the best approach to handling deductions is to shift this work to the responsible salesperson. This individual presumably visits customers on a regular basis, and so has the advantage of face-to-face meetings, which is less likely for the collection staff. Also, if deductions will impact a salesperson's commissions, this person will have an incentive to settle deductions in the company's favor. However, salespeople tend to oppose this approach on the grounds that it interferes with their ability to create new sales.

When all else fails and customers continue to take large deductions on a repetitive basis, it is time to seriously consider dropping them. This should involve a detailed review of the gross margin the company earns on business with that customer, less the amount of all deductions taken and all related deduction review and processing costs. Even if the result clearly calls for dropping the customer, it is best to first pass this information up to the company president, who may want to discuss the problem with his or her counterpart at the customer before finally authorizing the elimination of all credit sales to the customer.

(c) OUTSOURCING COLLECTIONS. It is always less expensive to collect receivables with an in-house staff, because there is no additional profit added to the collection department's efforts, as is the case with a collection agency. However, it is sometimes worthwhile to outsource certain functions to an agency because they tend to have experienced collectors, better access to information about some customers, and may know more about certain industries. This section discusses the types of outsourcing possibilities and when they should be used.

The basic concept when outsourcing to a collection agency is to hand over invoices for which the in-house collection team has been unable to collect payment, on the assumption that giving them to someone else for one last collection attempt is better than giving up and writing off the invoices. If the collection agency brings in some money from a customer, it typically takes a percentage of the received amount (one fourth to one third is typical) and remits the remainder to the company. Thus, a collection agency is generally treated as a last resort. However, they provide other services that may make them more attractive; for example, they can just issue dunning letters on the company's behalf, or collect NSF checks, or collect credit information on new customers. Depending on the workload of one's in-house collection staff, some or all of these alternatives may make sense, even to the point of handing over all small accounts receivable for collection as soon as they become late, simply because the in-house staff is not large enough to pursue any collection activities at all.

There are several factors to look for when reviewing new collection agencies. One is their ability to provide integrated legal services. This can streamline the collection process considerably, since a collection agency otherwise has a tendency to sit on invoices it cannot collect. By having immediate access to legal recourse, a collection agency is more likely to obtain payment from a customer. Another selection criterion is references—some collection agencies are exceptionally good, but this is hard to discern unless one talks to a number of references to determine their experiences with the agency. A third factor is fees; a common rate charged is one third of the amount collected, or even one half for smaller items such as retrieval of deductions. However, when evaluating based on fees, also consider the agency's success rate. If an agency costs a great deal but collects on most unpaid invoices, this is still a bargain. Finally, it may make sense to select an agency if it specializes in one's industry. It may have built up a considerable database of contacts within one's customers, as well as have a knowledge of their businesses, allowing them to obtain payments more readily.

If there are quite a few receivables to be sent to a collection agency, consider using several agencies at once. By doing so, one can compare their results to see which one performs best, and then shift more business to that agency in the future. It is also useful to compare the fees of each agency to their results. Further, by letting collection agencies know that they are competing with others, they tend to be more proactive in making collections in order to keep the company's business. Conversely, retaining the services of a single collection agency tends to make it complacent, resulting in worse collection performance.

No matter which agency is chosen, be sure to verify that it is bonded, and keep doing so at regularly scheduled intervals. This gives the company some recourse if an agency employee steals funds intended for the company. Also, track the regularity of remitted funds to the company. Some agencies operating on minimal working capital will retain collected funds for a long time, even though they are contractually obligated to remit them to the company as soon as they are received. Further, investigate at once if a customer complains about the collection activities of a collection agency; it is theoretically possible for the company to be legally responsible for the activities of an agency, since it is collecting on behalf of the company in an agent role.

Overdue accounts receivable are more difficult to collect for every additional day that passes by. This is a particular problem for collection agencies, since they are not normally given invoices by a client until they are well past due. To keep this from becoming a problem, the collection manager should have an organized process in place for making a determination as soon as possible about whether an invoice should be referred to a collection agency. This should involve working the customer through a standard series of collection techniques—if they all fail, refer the invoice at once and let a collection agency try to collect while the invoice is still reasonably "fresh."

An alternative to outsourcing is to create an in-house collection agency. By doing so, collectors can threaten to send an account out for collection, and then actually do so by passing the account across the aisle to the in-house agency, which operates under a different name and actually appears to customers to be a separate agency. Most customers do not like having their accounts sent to an agency and are more likely to pay when this happens. The company also avoids having to pay the large contingent fee that a real agency would demand. To make this ploy work, register the name of the in-house agency, give it a separate phone line and post office box address, and even consider setting it up legally as a different company. At a minimum, track its financial results as a separate department to see if it is a more profitable proposition than using an outside agency.

Pages 562–564. ***Delete Section 27.4: "Collections Task."***

CHAPTER 28

PLANNING AND CONTROL OF INVENTORIES

Page 571. *Replace Section 28.1 with the following:*

28.1 INTRODUCTION (REVISED)

Controlling a company's investment in inventory requires a considerable knowledge of the ordering, receiving, storage, picking, production, and shipping processes. This chapter focuses on specific issues within all of these areas that a controller can use to improve internal inventory-related systems, as well as to budget for inventory with a reasonable degree of accuracy. Please note that one should not use this chapter as a resource for making wholesale changes throughout a company; on the contrary, inventory is impacted by a number of interlocking systems, so each change must be planned in anticipation of what it will do to other parts of the company, such as machine utilization and customer service levels.

Page 573. *Add the following new sections after 28.2:*

28.2A INVENTORY PURCHASING (NEW)

Key factors in the purchase of inventory arise well before the production date, extending back into the product design process. There are other key purchasing factors involving communication levels, the distance to supplier locations, planning issues, and the frequency of deliveries that all have a major impact on the level of inventory one must maintain within a company. This section addresses all these issues.

By far the most common new-product design process is to design an entire product using an in-house design team, and then ask suppliers to bid on portions of the resulting design. However, suppliers could have advised the design team to use different materials or components that would have resulted in the same performance specifications at a lower total price. Consequently, it is frequently worthwhile to include suppliers in the design process, which they will be willing to do as long as they are promised some portion of the resulting business.

Suppliers can also tell if some components are very difficult to procure and can advise the design team to avoid them if at all possible. Otherwise, the company's ability to manufacture the products at all, or at least within a reasonable price range, will be in doubt. If there are no suppliers available for this kind of advice, the design team should consult with the purchasing department to see if they will have problems obtaining certain items. If some items must be included in a design but are difficult to obtain, the purchasing department can at least be used to purchase supplier capacity in advance, thereby locking down key sources.

It may also be possible to reduce in-house safety stock levels simply by shrinking the delivery lead times assigned to suppliers. Safety stock is essentially designed to cover a company's interim needs while it places an order with a supplier and waits for the order to arrive. In many cases, suppliers have sufficient on-hand stocks of some goods to ship faster than is currently the case, or can work with the company's industrial engineers to find ways to hasten their delivery times. However, this approach does not work well when some final assembly or customization is required before a supplier can ship a product.

Some suppliers have order lead times of many days or weeks. If the company alters an order inside that time frame, the supplier may have a difficult time filling the order in a timely manner. To avoid this problem, consider freezing the short-term production schedule for a sufficient duration to give suppliers sufficient notice to make changes outside of their minimum lead times. This can be difficult if suppliers have extremely long lead times, possibly necessitating the use of other suppliers with shorter lead times.

A major problem with obtaining goods from suppliers occurs when they are completely jammed with competing orders from multiple customers. In this situation, the company is forced to wait for its turn in the supplier's production process, and so must keep larger quantities of safety stock on hand until it receives replenishments. If the company requires large quantities of a predictable flow of goods, it can reduce this problem by purchasing blocks of supplier capacity. This essentially means that it buys the productive capacity of some portion of the supplier's manufacturing space, so that no one else can use it. This vastly improves the company's supply situation, resulting in far less need for safety stock. Also, in case the company's needs occasionally decline, one can even sell some of the capacity back to the supplier, who can then use it to service the needs of other customers.

Part of the time delay involved in ordering is the approval of orders within the company. If this requires multiple days, the inventory planning staff must plan for additional quantities of safety stock to ensure that supplies do not run out during this approval phase. Consequently, to reduce safety stock levels, consider either eliminating any form of approval for replenishment orders, or at least creating a more streamlined approval process. The only acceptable reason to have an approval for a repeating purchase is to ensure that orders are not being issued for items that are scheduled for termination. This can be more easily achieved by turning on a product termination flag in the item master file in the computer system.

A good way to reduce safety stocks is to order from suppliers located as close to the company as possible. By doing so, delivery transit times become minuscule, allowing one to keep very small safety stocks on hand to cover what may be just a few hours of production time until a replenishment arrives. This is a long-term approach to sourcing, since some very fine suppliers may be located far away, and will require considerable time to replace.

In-house inventory needs may decline even further by requiring suppliers to make multiple deliveries to the company each day. This drops the need for inventory to just a few hours' worth of stock. To avoid excessive paperwork, this approach works best if there is a long-term purchase order against which the company schedules a series of small product releases each day. At a more advanced level, one can even require suppliers to deliver directly into the production area, eliminating the need for any movement of inventory from the receiving dock to an intermediate storage area, and from there to the production floor. However, making this work requires the presence of receiving docks close to the production area, the communication of a firm inventory requirements schedule to suppliers on a regular basis, high levels of product quality being delivered, and the presence of key suppliers just a short distance away. Given these requirements, obtaining multiple deliveries per day can be difficult to implement.

If a company wants to adopt multiple daily deliveries of products, it must switch to sole sourcing. Otherwise, it becomes extremely difficult to manage the flow of many deliveries of the same product from multiple suppliers. Also, this approach calls for the use of streamlined accounting wherein suppliers are paid based on the total quantity of goods used in the production process; if there are several suppliers involved, it is impossible to tell whose goods were used, and therefore how much to pay which supplier.

It may be possible in limited situations for suppliers to retain ownership of their goods once they are shipped into the company's warehouse. The company pays for them only when they are extracted from the supplier's designated storage area on the premises, presumably to be sent to the production area. By using this approach, a company can reduce some working capital requirements by putting the onus of inventory storage on its suppliers. This approach is more attractive to suppliers when they are offered sole source status for the goods in question. However, suppliers must now increase their investment in inventory, while also spending more time monitoring and replenishing inventory levels, so they are likely to increase prices charged in order to compensate for these issues.

If there are a great many suppliers, it is possible that a company does not have enough purchasing expertise to deal with them all, or management feels that it can invest company funds more profitably in other areas than purchasing. If so, it may make sense to assign the role of lead supplier to a few suppliers, and have them handle the purchasing task for a large number of subcontractors. This approach works best for very complex products requiring large subassemblies for which lead suppliers can be assigned responsibility. Though lead suppliers are likely to charge extra for this service, they are also essentially guaranteed a larger proportion of the company's business, and so may be more willing to do it for only a modest price increase.

28.2B INVENTORY RECEIVING AND SHIPPING (NEW)

The shipping and receiving function requires the bulk of all warehouse staff time, as well as a great deal of warehouse space in which to break down and put away deliveries and marshal shipments for placement on trucks. Thus, receiving and shipping involve a considerable investment in both inventory and labor. This section describes a number of ways to improve the efficiency of this key area.

A major receiving problem is the treatment of unplanned receipts. These are items for which someone in the company has placed a verbal purchase order, so there is no record in the computer system of its existence. Since the receiving staff has no idea what it is, they park it to one side and send out a general notice, to which someone will hopefully respond in a few days, giving them some clue regarding where it should be sent within the company. This approach consumes both storage space and the time of the receiving staff. A better approach is to automatically reject all unplanned receipts at the point of delivery, with no exceptions. This will initially cause trouble within the company, since some of the verbal orders may be for critical items. Nonetheless, this is an appropriate action to take once a reasonable amount of warning has been given to the rest of the company.

The receiving area can become clogged with inventory, which not only requires more staff time in which to find needed items, but also calls for more warehouse space and can result in damage to any items improperly stored out in the open. To avoid this problem, the warehouse manager can require supplier deliveries only during certain hours of the day, and then cluster most of the warehouse staff in the receiving area during that time, thereby focusing all attention on the put-away function for a brief period of time. It is also helpful to deepen the receiving area in front of the dock doors, so there is sufficient space for the receiving staff to sort through deliveries as they arrive. This approach calls for the presence of sufficient warehouse staff and material movement equipment to handle deliveries, which calls for advance planning of received quantities, preferably several weeks in advance.

The efficient put-away of received goods can be accelerated through the use of advance shipping notices. Such notices can be a simple phone call from a shipper, as well as by fax, e-mail, or an electronic data interchange transmission. Whatever the communication medium, the intent is to forewarn the warehouse manager regarding the approximate arrival time of a delivery and the contents of the truck. This allows for much better put-away planning wherein docks can be set aside for specific trailers based on the shortest in-house travel time to put away their contents. Competent shippers will generally comply with a request for advance shipping notices, though smaller shippers will require considerably more training.

When items arrive at the receiving dock, the warehouse staff is not under a specific deadline to put away all the items, while it may be under considerable time pressure to pick and deliver items once they are ordered. Given this disparity, it may make sense to take somewhat more time in the receiving area to repackage received items into the quantities most commonly ordered by customers. By doing so, it will take much less time to fill orders. This approach works best if there is a great deal of excess space in the receiving area in which repackaging can be done.

An advanced form of an efficient put-away function is to stage received goods for put-away within designated zones. Under this approach, the receiving staff uses more space in the receiving area to break down deliveries into clusters small enough to be put away in a specific warehouse area (zone), which cuts down on the travel time of the put-away staff, allowing them to return to the receiving area more quickly to pick up another load. This approach is most cost-effective when the warehouse is so large that travel times are very long.

Less efficient receiving operations will pile up all the documentation related to items that have just been put away, and enter them all into the receiving computer in one large batch at the end of the day. The problem is that some of the goods may already have been sent to the production area or shipped back out to suppliers, while pickers are already attempting to find newly received items on the warehouse shelves. Further, it is impossible for cycle counters to make accurate inventory counts if some of the items they are counting are not yet present in the computer system. For all these reasons, it is best to log in all items as soon as they are received. This data entry effort is much easier if the warehouse staff is equipped with radio-frequency terminals that allow them to complete data entry tasks from anywhere in the warehouse.

The ultimate in improving receiving efficiency is to have no receiving function at all. To do so, the engineering department must have precertified the quality level of every supplier, while the purchasing department has arranged with them to make inventory deliveries directly to the production area for immediate use. This implies extremely low inventory levels, just-in-time deliveries, and the complete elimination of the warehouse area. All these preexisting conditions make it extremely rare to achieve the complete elimination of the receiving function. More commonly, a few suppliers are certified to bypass the receiving function, while a reduced receiving staff is still available to handle a smaller volume of incoming goods.

Shipped items are typically loaded onto pallets by hand, shrink-wrapped, and loaded onto a truck for delivery. The packaging involved in a shipment may not be necessary if the customer breaks open the pallets prior to the put-away step. If so, consider contacting the customer to see if a reusable container system might make more sense, such as returnable wheeled containers. Though there may be considerable up-front expense associated with the containers, the elimination of all other packaging materials may make this a cost-effective option.

The shipping function does not end at the dock door. The shipping manager should also be responsible for finding those freight companies with the best performance, both in terms of minimal damage to shipments and the ability to make deliveries on time. This may result in a reorientation away from using the lowest-cost shippers, instead requiring the use of a shipper evaluation system to determine which shippers are to be used. Otherwise, customers may require inventory on very short notice to replace either damaged goods or goods that have not arrived by the required due dates; this can severely impact a company's shipment schedule and its freight costs.

28.2C INVENTORY STORAGE (NEW)

There are many ways to improve the storage of inventory, beginning with the complete bypassing of the warehouse area and proceeding through better warehouse organization to zone storage and the use of special racking systems. This section discusses multiple options in each of these areas.

The best inventory storage option is not to store it at all. This can be done through the use of drop-shipping, whereby the company contacts a supplier and requests that it send goods straight to a customer, thereby completely bypassing the corporate storage facility. This approach requires the cooperation of the supplier, who may like to ship only in large quantities and so is less than enthusiastic about odd-sized shipments or deliveries that must be repackaged to appear to have come from the company instead. Also, the company's accounting department must have a system in place to obtain shipping notice from the supplier and issue a billing to a customer at that time, rather than the more common process of having the in-house shipping department trigger an invoice. Further, this approach works only if the goods being shipped require no additional transformation by the company through its own production process. A final complication is that a multiline order by a customer may call for deliveries from multiple suppliers, resulting in many deliveries to the customer, who may not appreciate the lack of a consolidated shipment. For all these reasons, one can rarely obtain the full benefits of drop-shipping.

If drop-shipping is not possible, consider cross-docking it instead. Under this approach, supplier deliveries come into the warehouse through one dock door and are immediately shifted across the warehouse to an outbound truck for delivery to a customer. This approach calls for no on-site storage in a formal racking system at all, and results in very fast inventory turnover. However, the warehouse function must be extremely well organized to match inbound and outbound deliveries within short time periods. It may also require the repackaging of delivery quantities to match the outbound requirement, as well as the relabeling of goods that have just arrived from a supplier. Further, one may require a great many dock doors to support the large number of trailers that may sit at the warehouse, waiting to be filled. Nonetheless, many companies have achieved considerable success with the cross-docking concept.

Another way to eliminate inventory from the warehouse is to distribute it to floor-stock locations in the production area. This tends to involve fittings and fasteners, which are the most labor-intensive inventory items to track and replenish anyway. The production staff loves this approach, since they no longer have to requisition these items from the warehouse. The primary difficulty with the use of floor stock is that they are no longer covered by the formal inventory tracking system, so there is no computerized way to automatically determine when an item should be reordered. Instead, someone must be assigned the task of manually reviewing floor-stock levels and placing orders with suppliers. It may be possible to assign this task to suppliers, who must visit the company frequently to replenish goods.

A key element of inventory storage is reducing the complexity of the storage system, so it is as easy as possible to find an item within the warehouse. The most basic way to do this is to assign a unique bin code to every bin in the warehouse, and to record in a computer system which inventory items are stored within each bin. A way to further streamline the system is to periodically review the inventory storage records and consolidate inventory items into the smallest possible number of adjacent bins. This typically results in a modest number of inventory items in a readily accessible bin near the front of the warehouse and an overflow quantity stored in a less accessible area. This concept of bin tracking is the most fundamental and necessary of all inventory storage requirements. Though bin tracking requires plenty of staff time to update, it is impossible to operate a warehouse without it.

The theoretically correct approach to storing inventory is to park it in any open bin, thereby maximizing the use of all available bins. However, this can result in high-usage items being stored in a distant corner of the warehouse, which lengthens the travel time of inventory pickers. To avoid this problem, consider assigning fixed inventory locations at the front of the warehouse to the most heavily used inventory, forcing less used items into the nether regions of the warehouse. If used, be sure to periodically review inventory usage levels, since the demand for a high-usage item may decline over time, reducing the need for a fixed location. For example, a company dealing in the sale of seasonal goods must completely reshuffle its warehouse once sales shift into a new season, since the demand for items will change at easily predictable times of the year.

The allocation of selected inventory to specific locations can be much more formally structured into the ABC storage system. Under this approach, the 20 percent most heavily used inventory items (the *A* items) are stored in the most readily accessible locations in the warehouse, while the 30 to 40 percent next most heavily used items (the *B* items) are stored in the next most accessible areas, and all remaining items (the *C* items) are stored in the rear of the warehouse. This approach is extremely useful for cutting down on the travel time of the warehouse staff, who usually end up spending nearly all of their time in the *A* area. Also, one can alter the storage rack system so that *A* items are stored in the most easily accessible storage systems, such as carousels, while less frequently used items are stored in less expensive bulk storage systems.

If customers send the company some of their inventory for inclusion in finished goods, it can easily become mixed in with regular corporate inventory, resulting in excess inventory valuations associated with items that the company does not really own. To keep this problem from occurring, consider creating a segregated warehouse area for customer-owned inventory. Also, use different inventory item codes for this inventory to which zero costs are assigned, thereby ensuring that the inventory will not be accidentally overvalued.

Some companies take the concept of customer inventory segregation a step further and block out large chunks of the warehouse for the storage of all inventory that a specific customer may use, no matter who owns it. Though this approach tends to waste space, it has the advantage of imposing tighter controls over inventory intended for the use of the most important customers. This is a useful technique only for the largest customers with whom a company does a significant proportion of its total business.

A company should alter its inventory storage systems to meet the requirements of its inventory, as well as the type of picking system in use. For example, if inventory is perishable, the racking system should allow for put-aways on one side and picking from the other, so the oldest items must be picked first; gravity-flow and pallet-flow racks work best in this situation. Alternatively, if there are large quantities of items stored on pallets, it may be possible to avoid excess aisle space by storing them in double-deep racks, push-back racks, or stacking lanes. If inventory items are small, are not picked frequently, and space is at a premium, consider using moveable racking systems that compress aisle space. For the same types of inventory but when there is plenty of vertical space available, an alternative is to install a multistory manual picking system. If pickers must pick large quantities of items as rapidly as possible, it may make sense to install a carousel system that brings parts to them at a central picking station; this is an expensive storage alternative, so be sure to conduct a cost-benefit analysis before implementing it. Finally, in a limited number of situations one can remove cross-braces from storage racks, so the warehouse staff can more efficiently access the racks from both sides. This option is possible only in low-weight storage situations in which the structural integrity of the racks is not threatened.

Even the size of containers and their storage pattern can interfere with the effective storage of inventory. For example, if a storage bin is four feet high and each case stored in it is 10 inches high, then 8 inches of space at the top of each bin are going to waste. Depending on the contents of each container, it may make sense to alter their height to be either 12 inches (to fully store four stacked containers in the rack) or 8 inches (to fully store six stacked containers). Also, the container-stacking pattern on a pallet should match the dimensions of the pallet as closely as possible. Otherwise, the cubic volume of storage space may be underutilized. Further, if the stacking pattern results in containers overhanging the edge of the pallet, those containers are more likely to be damaged in transit.

28.2D INVENTORY PICKING (NEW)

One of the highest-volume activities involving a large number of warehouse employees is inventory picking. Given its importance, one should consider all methods for arriving at the most cost-effective way to remove inventory from storage and transport it either to the customer or the production area. This section discusses a number of possible picking methods.

The least efficient picking method is to hand a single order to a stock picker, who walks all over the warehouse, searching for the required parts. At the most basic level, this picking ticket should include a column containing the inventory locations in which each inventory item is located, thereby reducing the search time. With the location available, pickers can now take a group of single-line orders, manually sort them by inventory location, and pick a large number of these orders during one picking tour of the warehouse. If there are multiline picking tickets, consider sorting each ticket by inventory location, so the picker can sequentially pick items within the ticket while walking down each aisle.

If pickers are handling multiple orders at once during a single picking tour, extra labor is required at the end of each tour to sort through all the picked items and separate them into different kitting bins for order delivery. A better approach is to issue multibin kitting carts to the pickers, so they can pick into different bins on the spot, thereby eliminating further order sorting at the end of each tour. Though efficient, this approach will result in some order inaccuracy, since pickers may inadvertently place picked items in the wrong bin.

A kitting cart is also a useful platform for a portable scale. If a company has very small parts in stock that pickers must manually count, portable battery-powered scales are an excellent way to streamline the picking process. However, these scales are very expensive, so procure them only if there is a reasonable amount of picking time being wasted on small-part counting.

In more primitive picking environments where there is no computer system, customer orders are manually transferred to picking tickets, which introduces the risk that information will be incorrectly transferred from the order to the picking ticket. To avoid incorrect picks caused by this problem, consider using a photocopy of the original customer order as the picking ticket. If the customer order form's layout is not conducive to picking, consider altering the form.

Order pickers generally conduct picking tours based on the immediacy of an order due date. However, this may result in orders that could be concentrated into a full truckload delivery being broken into a number of more expensive partial truckloads. One can avoid this problem by summarizing orders to be shipped to the same general location in a single large picking tour. The main difficulty is that orders that would not normally be due yet are being picked in advance of orders for which the order date is more immediate.

Clustering orders into a single large picking tour is certainly a better use of picker time, but pickers may not have a thorough knowledge of the entire warehouse, and so conduct inefficient tours during which they spend extra time verifying that picked items are indeed the correct ones. An alternative is zone picking, whereby pickers are assigned small portions of the warehouse. A zone picker is usually responsible for maintaining a specific warehouse area, and so not only has an excellent knowledge of its contents, but can slot items within the zone for maximum picking efficiency. By shifting partially completed orders from zone to zone, the overall efficiency and accuracy of the picking process tends to improve substantially. However, this usually calls for the use of some computerization and a conveyor belt to move orders from zone to zone.

In picking environments where inventory is hard to handle, pickers must remember to record each transaction after having used both hands to move the picked item, which tends to result in a great deal of missed pick transactions. To avoid this problem, consider using voice picking, whereby each picker wears a headset over which the computer system issues commands in a synthetic voice to pickers, telling them where to go for the next pick and what to remove from each bin. Pickers communicate back to the computer by voice, which is translated by the computer into electronic transactions. Voice picking works best in lower-volume picking environments without an excessive amount of background noise.

Where there is a high volume of picking transactions, consider using a pick-to-light system. Under this approach, an information display is attached to the front of each storage bin, with a direct linkage back to the picking module of one's inventory tracking system. When the system requires a pick, a light flashes on the display as well as a number indicating the quantity to pick. When the pick is complete, the picker presses a button on the display unit to indicate completion of the task. This approach works well when item dimensions are very small and where broken-case picking by hand is the norm. While this is a very good picking system with a low rate of transaction error, it is also expensive to install and so is used only for items subject to a high picking rate.

Though several picking methods have been noted that involve more efficient picking of multiple orders at once, they do not allow for the rapid picking of specific customer orders. If a customer is in a rush to receive a specific order, these picking methods are not the best way to fill the order. Instead, have an experienced picker do nothing but pick emergency orders from stock. This approach improves customer service at the expense of greatly reduced picking efficiency, so one should strongly consider charging the customer a picking fee to offset the loss of efficiency.

No matter what picking method is used, it is difficult to do so effectively if there are both pickers and put-away staff clogging the warehouse aisles at the same time. There are two ways to avoid this problem. First, install gravity-feed flow-through racking, so the put-away staff load parts into one side of a rack and the inventory rolls downhill for access by pickers on the other side. Second, have the put-away staff work a different shift than the pickers.

It is much easier to pick high-volume items when they are concentrated in one section of the warehouse. However, usage patterns will change over time, so be sure to periodically schedule a review of item usage to determine which items should be moved into or out of the high-volume picking areas.

28.2E PRODUCTION ISSUES IMPACTING INVENTORY (NEW)

Certain facets of a company's production system can impact the amount of inventory needed to run it, such as pay systems, equipment maintenance, and the configuration of equipment within the factory. Careful attention to these factors, as explained in this section, can drop the required inventory investment by a substantial amount.

A company's production bonus plan can result in too much inventory. This occurs when the incentive pay system has employees cranking out massive quantities of inventory in order to meet stretch bonus goals. This can be a problem if there is no room in which to store the excess inventory created by the workers, so consider using such bonus plans only for bottleneck operations in which there is never enough inventory being produced. A further problem with bonus plans is the propensity of workers to reduce the quality of their work in favor of more production volume. If this becomes an issue, consider issuing bonus reductions for low quality levels. Finally, consider eliminating production-based bonus plans entirely and converting to a just-in-time production system, where the emphasis is on manufacturing only what is needed.

Having an imbalance between the number of shifts worked in different parts of a factory can increase the level of work-in-process (WIP) inventory. For example, one area may have two shifts and all other areas just one shift, so the one multishift area piles up completed inventory for eight hours before the next downstream area arrives for work and can begin processing it. Even if the multishift area is working extra hours because it is a bottleneck operation, it may still be feasible to run smaller skeleton crews in other production areas in order to begin processing WIP as soon as it becomes available, thereby reducing the total level of WIP in the facility.

If a factory is built around a small number of high-volume machines, it is likely that it requires a substantial amount of WIP inventory. This problem arises because a single, very expensive machine must be run at all times in order to justify the company's investment, resulting in a buffer of raw materials stored in front of it and partially processed inventory after it. Further, large and complex machines tend to break down or require more maintenance, so the production scheduling staff tends to build up inventory buffers against the eventuality that the machine will go down. To avoid these problems, consider replacing a single large machine with several smaller and less complex ones. This approach yields less total maintenance downtime and also the flexibility to shift work among several machines.

It is better not only to use smaller machines in the production area, but also to schedule smaller production runs on those machines. A large and complex machine necessitates the use of infrequent, lengthy equipment setups, followed by long production runs to justify the setup time. This results in large amounts of finished goods that must be stored until sold. A better approach is to use smaller, inexpensive equipment that can be easily set up for new production runs, thereby making it cost-effective to have production runs of as little as one unit, which in turns reduces downstream inventory levels to a remarkable extent. Further, very small production runs allow downstream workstation operations sufficient time to inspect each incoming part and tell the upstream machine operator if they have just produced an item that is out of specification. This immediate quality review creates such a rapid feedback loop that very little inventory must be scrapped during the production process.

Equipment downtime is a major reason why WIP inventory tends to build up. When a machine goes down for any length of time, the WIP scheduled to be processed through it either sits until repairs are completed or is routed to another machine whose capacity may not be sufficient to process it in the short term. Further, the inventory planning staff may build up an expectation of considerable machine downtime, and so always plans for more inventory than is really needed. There are a number of ways to reduce these issues. First, create and follow a detailed machine maintenance plan, whereby equipment is serviced during nonproduction periods. Also, implement a preventive maintenance program, so machines are less likely to fail. Next, purchase as many machines as possible from the same manufacturer, so the maintenance staff does not require as much knowledge of different machines in order to effect repairs. This may also result in less spare parts inventory if the supplier uses many of the same parts on different machines. Finally, train the production staff to take care of minor repairs on their own. All these steps can reduce machine downtime.

Even machines that appear identical on the outside will require varying levels of fine-tuning before parts produced on them fall within specifications, due to varying levels of machine wear and tear. For this reason, the production setup staff tends to waste raw materials while it conducts lengthy test runs on new production runs. To avoid wasting inventory, consider scheduling production runs only on the same machines every time, and storing the exact machine settings to create those parts. It then becomes easier to initially set up each machine with few or no subsequent alterations to create perfect parts.

A major cause of WIP inventory buildup within the production area is the presence of aisles. A machine operator on one side of an aisle must complete enough work to fill up a pallet, at which point a forklift operator shifts the pallet across the aisle to the next workstation. The pallet-load of stock can be eliminated simply by running a conveyor across the aisle, so the first machine operator can roll stock directly to the next machine. This approach can eliminate a large amount of inventory while also giving industrial engineers the opportunity to shrink the production area by eliminating aisles.

The most efficient use of inventory is achieved when a production planning staff schedules production levels to match either the in-house or expected quantity of inventory. However, when customers order items at the last possible minute, this throws off the scheduling process, resulting in too much on-hand inventory in some areas and the incurrence of overnight delivery charges to bring in other items needed to fulfill the rush orders. Further, expeditors must walk orders through the production and warehouse areas, leaving a considerable disturbance in their wakes. To eliminate these problems, consider refusing customer orders that fall within the minimum scheduling period set by the production planning staff. If a customer is an important one and insists on immediate service, then charge such a stiff premium that the customer will at least scale back its demands for short-term service and the company will be well compensated for its expediting assistance.

28.2F INVENTORY TRANSACTIONS (NEW)

There can be an enormous number of inventory transactions—recording initial receipt, quality review, put-away, picking, and delivery either to customers or the shop floor, depending on the transaction. This is an area rife with errors, especially if the staff must manually log all entries into a computer system. This section describes a number of techniques for reducing the inventory transaction error rate.

One of the simplest improvements is to eliminate any data entry backlogs. When a number of transactions are not entered at once, the on-hand quantities of inventory can become inaccurate, making it very difficult to plan purchasing and production activities, as well as cycle counting. To eliminate backlogs, management should emphasize its importance in the warehouse manager's job review. Also, consider additional data entry training for the warehouse staff, as well as dedicating one person to nothing but data entry (which also tends to reduce data entry errors).

Another simple error correction technique is to run an inventory-on-hand quantity report every day and search it for negative inventory balances. When found, investigate the underlying transactions causing the negative balance, and correct these problems. This approach works best if there is easy access in the computer system to all inventory transactions, along with the date and time when they were created and who entered them. This additional information is critical for tracking down problems.

Another way to spot transaction problems is to cycle-count the inventory, so that someone is constantly comparing on-hand to book inventory balances. The key activity here is not finding discrepancies but rather investigating why they occurred. Continuous cycle-counts put ongoing emphasis on bombproofing transactions, so the number of errors should decline precipitously if this approach is followed.

A primary cause of inventory transaction errors is manual data entry. Given the sheer volume of transactions, it is almost impossible not to have errors. One way to avoid the problem is to use bar codes. Under this approach, a bar code is added to a product as soon as it arrives at the receiving dock, detailing the item description, quantity, and unit of measure. As long as the information contained in the bar code is correct, all subsequent scans of this information will be correct as well. The concept can be taken a step further by bar-coding all inventory locations. By doing so, one can eliminate nearly all manual entries from inventory transactions.

Even bar-coding can cause problems if scanned information is being stored in handheld units carried by the warehouse staff and downloaded to the central computer only at the end of their shifts. Under this approach, information may be updated with as much as an eight-hour delay. A much better alternative is to issue radio-frequency scanners to the warehouse staff, so any scanned transactions are immediately transferred by radio transmission to a receiver that is linked to the central computer system. Though wireless scanning units are expensive, this is an excellent way to ensure real-time entry of inventory transactions.

If a wireless system is installed, one can consider shifting to the ultimate in warehouse systems—a warehouse management system. This is a computerized system that runs all warehouse functions in the most efficient manner possible by issuing commands to the wireless terminals being carried by the warehouse staff. It tells them where to put away inventory items based on their usage patterns, where pickers should go to obtain inventory while walking the shortest possible distance, where incoming trailers should dock in order to shorten the put-away time from them to the warehouse racks, and so on. Warehouse management systems are quite expensive and are therefore cost-effective for only the largest warehouse systems.

28.2G INVENTORY QUANTITY MANAGEMENT (NEW)

There are many ways to reduce inventory levels through the inventory planning process while still maintaining high levels of customer service. These techniques are scattered throughout a company, encompassing product design, sales forecasting, management of the planning function, distribution systems, and the treatment of obsolete inventory. This section covers many possibilities in these areas that can lead to inventory reduction.

A major cause of inventory inflation is the use of a multitude of product options, which requires a company to stock some quantity of each product variation. Though this approach certainly gives customers a wide product range from which to choose, it is extremely common to also see high product obsolescence caused by some product configurations not selling as well as others. Thus, part of the design process is reducing the number of product options to a more tolerable level that reduces a company's inventory investment. One way to retain a large number of product configurations while still having small inventory levels is to build inventory only to a semifinished level, with all options added after customers place orders. This approach works only if the product design team is involved, since they must create products with "bolt-on" options.

Inventory levels can also be reduced by continually examining sales quantities for each product and eliminating those items whose sales have dropped below a minimum cutoff level. This approach is complex, since one must also consider retaining stock in sufficient quantities to cover expected replacements due to warranty claims or service issues. Also, some products may continue to be sold for longer than would normally be the case if this is the best way to eliminate some components from stock that are no longer being used in the manufacture of any other products.

Engineers like to design finely crafted products that operate properly only when high-tolerance components are used. However, components with tight tolerances may be difficult to produce or acquire, resulting in a great deal of scrap. Thus, it is better to work with the engineers to design products requiring lower-tolerance parts, so that a larger percentage of raw materials will work properly in their manufacture.

When customers order a product that is not available, they may take their business elsewhere rather than wait for the company to produce more stock. However, if the company maintains a list of substitute products, it may be able to ship one of the other items to the customer, thereby reducing its finished-goods inventory. This typically calls for an updated substitute product list to be maintained where the order entry staff can easily access it.

Senior management may have mandated a very high level of customer service, which is represented in the warehouse area by the continued presence of on-hand inventory for any product a customer may wish to order. However, this calls for a high level of inventory investment, which may in turn result in significant obsolete inventory if some items are never bought by customers. Consequently, it makes sense to periodically review the mandated customer service level with senior management, including in the discussion the cost of this policy in terms of incremental inventory investment.

High customer service levels may mandate a large safety stock for each finished-goods item. However, what if product demand is highly seasonal? Safety stock levels may still result in stock-outs during high-demand periods and excessive inventory during low-demand periods. To avoid this problem, consider scheduling periodic adjustments to safety stock levels for those inventory items known to have seasonal demand.

If there is a management directive to reduce the total investment in inventory, the production planning staff may have little time to do so, especially if there are thousands of parts in stock to be reviewed. A simple alternative is to reduce inventory levels for only the subset of items with high usage levels. The turnover rates on these items is so rapid that any reduction actions taken will be reflected in an inventory reduction in a very short period of time. Conversely, if inventory reduction actions were taken on slow-moving inventory, it could be months before there is any discernible impact on the total inventory investment. The planning staff can save more time in reducing inventory by using an in-house material requirements planning system to model the impact of changes in safety stock, lot sizes, or lead times on the total level of inventory investment.

A company may distribute inventory to customers from a number of regional warehouses. If so, it must stock a sufficient inventory quantity in each location to meet expected customer demand. An alternative is to centralize the storage of smaller or expensive items, so a smaller quantity can be stored in one location for distribution to all customers. This approach circumvents regional warehouses and their primary reason for existence—rapid delivery to customers—so be sure to centralize only those inventory items that can be reasonably inexpensively shipped by overnight delivery services directly to customers. This usually calls for a cost-benefit analysis to determine which inventory items should be treated in this manner.

A warehouse network is designed to ship inventory in the most economical manner possible to regional customer clusters. Given this objective, warehouses must be carefully sited within each region for maximum effect. However, customers change over time, as does the quantity of their purchases, so one should occasionally rationalize the warehouse network through a regularly scheduled warehouse analysis. This is not a frequent event, since a warehouse location must be clearly inefficient before a company should undertake the considerable expense required to move to a new location.

A key area in which to control inventory quantities is obsolete inventory. This can be done in the most organized manner by creating a materials review board, comprised of members of the production, engineering, purchasing, and accounting staffs, which review the inventory on a regular basis to determine the disposition of obsolete items. By creating a formal review system for inventory disposition, one can be sure that inventory is not being thrown away that might have been used in-house, while also ensuring that obsolete items are cleared out as soon as possible.

It can be difficult to identify obsolete inventory. One approach is to spot inventory to which inventory tags from the previous year's inventory count are still attached. Another way is to use a material requirements planning system to identify all inventory items for which there is no planned use. A third approach is to run a report comparing usage levels for the past year to the on-hand quantity to see if quantity reductions can be made. Finally, a simple visual review of each warehouse bin is likely to spot items that are covered in dust or have never been opened, or on which old shipment dates are still readable.

The typical ways to dispose of obsolete inventory include:

- Their planned inclusion in manufactured goods as a substitute material
- Selling them at a discounted price
- Donating them for a tax deduction
- Returning them to suppliers for a restocking fee
- Selling them to salvage contractors
- Having the service department sell them to customers under the guise of spare parts

Whatever approach is used, disposition can take a long time and requires considerable management oversight to ensure that it is completed in a timely manner. Also, be sure to grant the warehouse department a sufficiently large inventory write-off budget to allow it to dispose of all necessary items; otherwise, the warehouse area may contain clearly useless items for longer than necessary, on the grounds that management does not want their disposal to adversely impact the company's financial results.

28.2H WAREHOUSE LAYOUT (NEW)

A warehouse is not intended to be a large boxlike area into which inventory is stuffed. On the contrary, a great deal of planning is required to ensure that inventory is stored safely, with ready access, in such a way that the perishable items are used up in a first-in, first-out manner. Further, the storage system should result in maximized storage within the warehouse area. This section describes a number of techniques for achieving these goals.

A key management decision impacting the warehouse layout is what to do with excess inventory quantities during peak storage periods. Management may conclude that the main warehouse area will be configured for the largest possible amount of inventory. However, this may not be an effective investment of funds if the "normal" inventory carrying level is much lower. In many situations, it is more cost-effective to design a smaller central warehouse and then plan to store excess inventory in such temporary storage spaces as trailers or nearby warehouses.

There should be a number of storage areas within a warehouse. For example, all high-volume picking activities should be clustered in one area, which makes it easier to supervise the picking staff and also keep high-maintenance picking equipment close together. In addition, all bulk overflow storage should be kept at the furthest end of the warehouse from higher-volume activities, while such specialized storage as cold storage or high-value storage must be kept in a carefully controlled space. These general concepts imply the presence of storage zones devoted to particular types of inventory, rather than a variety of storage systems scattered throughout the facility.

When designing the best possible warehouse layout, be sure to integrate into the design the existence of all building supports. They should be enclosed within the racking system so that they are not protruding into aisles where workers and equipment must negotiate a way around them and risk damaging goods in transit.

A large amount of warehouse space is taken up by aisles. This is wasted space to the extent that they can be narrowed without endangering the safety of the warehouse staff. For example, adjust the width of aisles where pallets are stored to the maximum turning requirements of the forklifts intended for them. Alternatively, if only manual put-aways and picking are to be conducted, the aisle width can probably be narrowed to the minimum level required by local fire codes. If automated put-away and retrieval systems are to be used, then the aisle only has to be wide enough to contain the automated system. Further, there should always be inventory stored on both sides of an aisle, so never put an aisle adjacent to an outside wall—this is a poor use of space.

If aisles are used, the assumption is that people or machines will travel along them on a regular basis. However, some higher-volume warehouse areas are better served by conveyors, so that either people or machines are entirely occupied with picking inventory and placing it on the conveyor, rather than physically shifting goods to other locations. If a cost-effectiveness review reveals that conveyors should be installed, this means that aisle width must match the width of the conveyor while leaving sufficient room for pickers or maintenance staff to either side.

In extremely high-volume transaction areas where larger inventory items are being moved, it may make sense to install an automated storage and retrieval system (ASRS). This approach involves the installation of a multistory traveling robot system within an aisle; the robot automatically travels to a designated bin, removes the required pallet, and shifts it to a convenient pickup point. An ASRS is extremely expensive, though it can substantially reduce put-away and picking times.

One may walk through a warehouse and conclude that its design is excellent; however, look up and verify that storage racks go all the way to the ceiling. If not, all the vertical space above the existing racks is being wasted. To avoid this situation, install properly cross-braced racks that will safely handle loads up to a point just below the warehouse sprinkler system. Also, purchase forklifts capable of safely moving pallets into and out of the highest bins in an efficient manner. If there is no current need to fill this vertical space, then management has acquired excess storage space.

If there is a need for manual picking in some areas of the warehouse, this should be a consideration when laying out the picking area in relation to the amount of vertical space available in the warehouse. It is best to position such areas where the ceiling height is low, since pickers cannot effectively use space more than about seven feet high. Alternatively, if the entire ceiling area is high, consider a multilevel manual picking area to make use of the extra space.

If the engineering staff has engaged in a quality certification process with suppliers, it should eventually be possible to entirely eliminate the quality review area within the warehouse, or at least plan on its gradual reduction in size. This concept can be incorporated into the initial warehouse design, so one can plan to extend an existing racking system into the quality review area over time.

From an inventory control perspective, it may be necessary to lock down the warehouse area with fencing. This requirement is necessary when the manufacturing staff is in the habit of browsing the warehouse shelves to find parts they need for the latest production job. When they take items from stock without logging them out of the computer system, this throws off the inventory planning system. The need for fencing can be reduced by shifting smaller low-cost fittings directly into the production area, as well as by maintaining high levels of accuracy in kitting jobs for delivery to the shop floor. Nonetheless, it is probably necessary to plan on fencing in the more accessible warehouse areas until the overall production planning and control system improves sufficiently to make it unnecessary for anyone to want to remove items from the warehouse.

Finally, it is possible in rare situations to entirely eliminate the warehouse, thereby bypassing all discussion of the warehouse layout. To do so, shift as much inventory from the warehouse as possible to storage locations in the production area, and create an alternative manual system for determining when to replenish those stocks. Next, remove all obsolete inventory from the remaining warehouse storage area. Third and most difficult, certify suppliers for minimum quality levels and then have them deliver in small daily volumes directly to the production area. This should result in no need for a central storage area at all, unless there are extremely expensive or hard-to-obtain items required for production.

PART 6

COMPUTER SYSTEMS AND RELATED TECHNOLOGY

CHAPTER 41A*

MAINTAINING AND UPGRADING ERP FINANCIAL SYSTEMS (NEW)

41A.1 OVERVIEW

Enterprise resource planning (ERP) financial systems are generally mature, full featured, and provide a reasonable user interface. This is because the ERP vendors introduced their applications in the finance area, followed years later by the manufacturing and customer relationship management (CRM) applications. The largest players in this market space are SAP, Oracle, and PeopleSoft. All three vendors have gained thousands of customers over the past two decades. In parallel with their increasing market share has been a downward trend in cost for licenses and hardware to run the financial applications. As a result, thousands of installations took place, many of which had no road map for future maintenance and upgrades. This chapter will focus on the challenges and lessons learned related to postinstallation maintenance and upgrades of ERP financial systems.

41A.2 CURRENT STATE

Many companies have installed ERP financial applications without understanding how to take advantage of the features or functionality. Others have decided the cost to apply vendor-sponsored maintenance releases is

*This chapter was authored by Deborah Metzger, a manager at Deloitte in San Francisco, California.

too large. Finally, others have attempted to provide the business with real-time access to multiple years' worth of financial data without understanding the performance impact. In the end, these businesses have failed to rein in the costs associated with their ERP financial systems.

41A.3 KEY STRATEGIES TO MINIMIZE COST

As is the case with an automobile, the ERP financial system will fail to meet ongoing business requirements if it is not properly maintained. Eventually, it will break down and the cost to fix or start over may far exceed the ongoing maintenance costs. In addition to this continued requirement-wise lack of fit, the system will usually grow in size as the number of transactions increases.

Some of the key strategies to minimize the cost related to these issues include the following:

- *Understand the ERP vendor's strategy.* One of the key points to consider is the vendor's marketing strategy. What are they offering initially at the time of sale? How are they providing you with more features and functionality over time? Be aware of the fact that above all else, the ERP vendor wants to sell to you initially, and continue to sell to you as long as you own the software. The vendor also wants you to be faced with the need for its consulting services. Your awareness of these facts will allow you to better plan your cost minimization approach up front.
- *Develop a maintenance strategy.* ERP vendors continually release new features in the form of "patches" or "maintenance packs." It is sometimes difficult to understand which ones, if any, to implement. The more important thing to understand is the long-term cost if you fail to take any and are faced with desupport of your installed version. The recommended approach is to develop a long-term plan that involves continued maintenance. It will often be both painful and more costly to reinstall or apply multiple large maintenance upgrades than taking smaller upgrades over time due to the costs related to testing. Because the ERP financial systems are integrated, the more extensive the patch, the more testing

is required in multiple areas. For example, a small feature release for payables does not require testing assistance in receivables. An overall financial upgrade involves testing in every module, using most features.

- *Develop test plans and understand how to test.* While it is true that ERP systems are full featured, these features drive complexity. This complexity becomes apparent whenever new patches containing these features are applied and require testing from the business. Therefore, it is important to develop a series of finance test plans and data that can be used in the event that testing is required. Often, test cases are written specifically for a project or situation and include both the test and the data for the test. Separating the test data from the test case allows the test case to be reused. Careful thought related to test data allows the finance staff to be able to easily determine if the ERP system is impacted by the patch or subsequent upgrade. Testing should be performed with assistance from information technology (IT) where possible. Joint testing using both finance and IT staff allows finance to test "real" scenarios and allows IT to solve the related technical issues.
- *Develop a financial archive.* Regardless of whether you elect to adopt a more continual maintenance strategy, the size of your online ERP financial system will grow as time marches on. Financial data stored in the ERP system is paramount to understanding company performance. Unfortunately, none of the large ERP packages will perform well once they grow past a certain point. Normally, this is only one or two years for a $1 billion–type company. This conflicts with the need to access the information up to as much as 5 or 10 years at a time for reporting purposes. The recommended approach is to take advantage of the ERP vendor-provided purge and archive routines where available. A strategy to develop an offline data warehouse or reporting system will allow the financial staff to access this information over time. Be sure to request the ability to combine current (transaction-level) data with previous (archived and purged) data when you are designing your archive.

- *Desupport and the cost to the business.* Another component of the ERP vendor's marketing strategy is to eventually desupport its installed version to provide new features. What does this mean to finance? In two words, more cost. One way to minimize this cost is to be able to easily upgrade your financial system. If you have followed the preceding recommendations, your cost to upgrade will be minimized. The cost to begin your upgrade with large patches and purging data will rapidly deplete your budget. Reinstalling the ERP system from scratch may be your only alternative. If you have strategically applied patches, developed a mature set of test plans, understand how to test and what is important to test, and have purged your ledger and subledgers, upgrade time and complexity will most likely be reduced.
- *Extend, don't customize.* It is unrealistic to think that any ERP financial system will meet all of your business requirements. More importantly, the ERP vendor has developed its marketing strategy to prevent you from customizing its application. One of the major cost mistakes related to ERP financial systems is the decision to customize rather than extend the system using a vendor-supported approach. If you purchase the vendor's system and develop features that are not part of its system, each time you apply a patch that impacts that particular customization, you will be forced to either decline the new feature or ask IT to redevelop the customization. If you have developed an ongoing maintenance strategy such as the one presented above, if the ERP vendor elects to desupport your version, the cost to upgrade will be far less than if you had customized.
- *Attend the user group meetings.* ERP vendors sponsor biannual or annual user conferences where they present new features and lessons learned and review enhancement requests. These conferences are often the only opportunity for end customers to influence the vendor's feature strategy. Due to the maturity of the financial applications, the enhancement request groups for payables, receivables, general ledger, and fixed assets are organized and effective. Attendance in the new features and request sessions, along with meeting peers

who are using the ERP systems, provides you with the ability to influence the current and future state in the finance area. If nothing else, one of the conference white papers may provide you with the ability to use the system in a way that you did not even think of in thc past.

41A.4 CONCLUSION

There are various strategies finance can employ to reduce the costs associated with ongoing maintenance and upgrades to its ERP system. Once purchased, the ERP system can be costly to maintain. Developing an understanding of how these costs can grow over time is important to realize at the time of purchase. If the ERP system was purchased and has been running without respect to maintenance, the overall cost to upgrade or reimplement may far exceed plan. Learning from the mistakes of others will provide finance with the ability to realize the long-term benefits of the ERP application and reduce the overall cost.

CHAPTER 41B*

IMPACT OF ENTERPRISE APPLICATIONS ON FINANCE (NEW)

41B.1 HOW DO THESE DEPLOYMENTS AFFECT ME?

Enterprise-wide projects that touch and change your business processes should raise concerns and questions: How can your company continue selling its products and services when the systems are down? How will you report financial statements when you do not have sales figures? What is the impact of telling your stockholders and the board that you may receive a "qualified" audit evaluation because of the lack of systemic controls and your failure to comply with Sarbanes-Oxley?

This chapter focuses on what you can do from the finance organization perspective on very large projects that scale across the enterprise or cross international boundaries, changing processes, cultures, and their enabling technologies.

---

* This chapter was authored by Shinli H. Chi, CPA, and Ashlee Henry at Deloitte.

(a) DEFINITION OF ENTERPRISE IT PROJECTS. As companies synthesize technological advances into the mainstream, organizations are implementing more enterprise-wide projects using technology that either increase efficiency of operations through decreased costs or increase sales by understanding the relationships with their customers.

The scope of these technology implementations and business process changes should directly correlate to the benefit realized. The larger, global or enterprise-wide, projects tend also to provide the scale necessary to achieve the business case. We can classify most of the information technology (IT) projects as focused on either enterprise resource planning or customer relationship management.

(i) Enterprise Resource Planning (ERP). Enterprise resource planning focuses on internal operations and reporting systems—data warehousing or knowledge warehouses included—for example, aligning processes and their enabling technologies that facilitate manufacturing, supply chain, and accounting. Mainstream software applications synonymous with ERP are SAP, Oracle, and Peoplesoft. Organizations' primary reason for implementation of ERP is to lower cost through new functionality, automation, and efficiency.

(ii) Customer Relationship Management (CRM). Today, myriad definitions surround CRM. To properly capture the general idea, we define CRM as an external focus on interactions with your customer—focusing on all areas and processes that touch your customers (i.e., customer service, marketing, and campaign management). Mainstream software applications synonymous with CRM are Siebel, Salesforce.com, and Oracle. An organization's primary reason for implementing CRM is to increase its sales by understanding who its customer is, what the customer wants, and how to extend the relationship.

(b) WHY DEPLOY ENTERPRISE-WIDE IT SOLUTIONS TODAY? Organizations will turn to technology as their key strategy enabler for revenue enhancement, cost-reduction strategies of outsourcing and integration, and statutory compliance.

Organizations invest in technologies that enhance their revenue. Most spending from 2001 to 2003 was on CRM-based software applications that enable an organization to understand its customers and allow companies to serve more customer-tailored needs.

The other big push in this decade is outsourcing—from components of manufacturing to staff positions within finance, sales, and IT. Today, many organizations are taking advantage of outsourcing their nonstrategic functions to foreign locations, which provides attractive cost savings.

The key to these large technology investments is information. The information challenge is a vast ocean looking for a ship. Who is the owner? We know that oceans can support many ships. Rapid data growth and technology's assimilation of data requires integration to provide the required value and benefit needed in today's environment. Data is being captured in every function of the organization, and ability to share information from various functions is the value of integration—a requirement for today's enterprise applications (see Exhibit 41B.1).

The major accounting scandals over the past few years and the corresponding legislation (e.g., Sarbanes-Oxley) have forced companies to look into their ERP and CRM solutions for control. The major ERP and CRM solutions have historically done an outstanding job of offering business process and financial controls, but companies have not always chosen to implement all of what is offered or to keep a close watch on the controls' effectiveness. Companies are now revisiting their available controls and taking advantage of new tools offered by major software vendors (e.g., Oracle Internal Control Manager) and services offered by the major auditing firms (e.g., Deloitte Sarbanes-Oxley Integrated Services Offering).

EXHIBIT 41B.1 EXAMPLE OF HOW DATA CAN BECOME MORE MEANINGFUL WHEN SHARED

To take a customer order, we have listed sample data elements and you can see how these data items are an intrinsic part of the process and shared by various applications and their users.

Data Element	Data Application Owner	Functional User
Customer Name	ERP/CRM	Sales, Marketing, Credit, Receivables
Available to Promise (ATP)	ERP	Sales, Supply Chain Planning, and Manufacturing
Item	ERP	R&D, Supply Chain, Manufacturing, Pricing, Marketing

41B.2 PITFALLS

With organizations understanding their technology needs and implementing proven enterprise applications, what can go wrong?

Companies today have become more sophisticated in their technology needs. They understand the potential benefits associated with the technology as well as the complications with implementation. Most companies have learned about the implementation risks associated with enterprise applications. In fact, large organizations even employ consultants to help with their deployment and reduction of implementation risk. What risks are still left on the table? All of them.

From a finance perspective, implementing enterprise applications is similar to performing open heart surgery. Even though critical processes seemingly escape the operation, they can be impacted by the technology in related areas. Consider the following example:

On a global implementation of sales agreements and order management, whereby new technologies would replace the old yet preserve the organization's current sales process, the technology implemented failed after going into production by dropping orders between the front-end order capture system and the back-office systems that stayed relatively the same. All of finance's processes and systems remained the same. The only difference was that the new front-end order capture system would send orders to the back-office application for processing and accounting. The system passed many rounds of testing and was certified by the businesses prior to going live. What happened?

Under real production environments, outside factors such as customer records were unsynchronized due to timing between the front-end and back-office applications. The sales made never got to the back office to be recognized. Finance did not even know until the business controller realized that the revenue figures seemed to be too low. As the quarter end approached, the finance organization struggled to understand the sales system and find the "lost" revenue.

Enterprise applications, even when integrating various packages (i.e., Siebel CRM, Oracle ERM, and Peoplesoft HR/PR), share key master data on which all relationships are founded. In the preceding example, to take an order, the customer record is shared across multiple functions spanning applications.

Various case studies have shown that even with the best processes and enabling technologies, the most fundamental element of information—*data*—can impair the multimillion-dollar investments in technology.

A well-known high-tech company in Silicon Valley invested over $300 million to implement CRM and ERP systems worldwide to replace their antiquated systems with the latest Siebel and Oracle system. Even after hiring the best consultants on the market and spending more than two years transforming its business processes, data idiosyncrasies kept haunting and preventing the organization from realizing the true benefits of the system.

Customer data issues can extenuate the turnover time, increase cost to research, and result in lost revenue due to impacted pricing rules. The impact externally is even greater, when you consider the possible loss of customers caused by not recognizing who they are, nor treating them appropriately or timely due to incorrect records or increased turnaround time to respond to simple questions.

Who owns the data? Relational databases serve as the foundation for most of the business applications tying data elements of customer to business terms. These growingly complex data models and relationships have effectively supported the business process reengineer's focus of business process. Business processes form a holistic end-to-end point of view spanning many corporate functions and users. For example, the order-to-cash process spans sales to supply chain to finance.

The question is: Who is responsible? Who owns the information? Who owns the data? The answer is that all data is shared to support the process-oriented business structures. However, each specific function may emphasize a different perspective of the data in assimilating information important to them.

For example, who owns the customer? Does the sales organization own the customer? Sales would drive the definition of customer to track distribution information, market elements, and transactional information like shipping destination and sales representative information.

What about finance? Finance would define the credit allocation and review of the customer. Finance would also own definition of revenue recognition rules, receivable terms to monitor bad debt, the billing address, and various other elements.

An enterprise application delivers a system that encompasses the various business functions that cross each process end to end, streamlining and linking the various pieces together. Thus, under the usual circumstances, each area interrelates, creating dependencies and seemingly hidden impacts. There are no assurances that risk is automatically manageable by considering a proven package or noticing scope overlap with finance and accounting. Understanding that data is easily fragmented by business users but should be considered as a whole in terms of a uniform model, the key mitigation is cross-functional communication.

41B.3 WHAT LEADS TO AN INCREASED RISK PROFILE?

What constitutes an increased risk profile? First, based on implementation and deployment experience, multiple elements compose the fatal mistake. The opportunity to prevent the mistake may present itself many times. We have identified the top three factors from a finance perspective that contributed to unsuccessful enterprise application deployments.

(a) TRADITIONAL FINANCE AND ACCOUNTING ROLE. Historically, finance and accounting line up as staff functions supporting the business by being the company scorekeepers. Accounting and finance understand the basic business functions of marketing, sales, operations, and distribution. More to the point, as accountants, we quantify each transaction and qualify each account. However, finance and accounting's scope stopped at recording financial transactions.

Even though finance understands each function and its role in the corporation machine, it is neither their job nor in their scope of responsibilities to understand or interact at a level more than just transactional accounting.

Accountants often fail to recognize the size of the impacts across interdependent transactional data, or how seemingly nonfinance or -accounting functions directly impact the bottom line.

For example, for a global enterprise that implemented a new distribution system, on the fulfillment process we encountered a growing issue that grew unchecked until quarter end. The conversion scripts correctly brought over the inventory balances; however, this same script misplaced some of the product, meaning that the product ended up at a location different from where the system said.

As logistics filled the orders, they encountered a system problem. The system would not allow them to fill the order, because at that location no inventory existed. Revenue and cost of goods sold were not recognized because the order could not be shipped and completed.

Logistics staff scrambled to compensate. Eventually, they figured out that they could initiate a receipt of product into inventory (e.g., the missing product) and then record the shipment and complete the order, when actually the physical shipment had already been shipped. Moreover, upon receipt, the application asks which account to charge. The only account that seemed to be appropriate was an adjustment account that was a contra-expense—thereby doubling the revenue.

At the quarter end, the controllership asked why this adjustment account had such a high balance. The organization began to realize that some sort of error occurred—not just an ordinary misclassification, but one that negatively impacted their revenue and left them in jeopardy as the audit of counts and Sarbanes-Oxley began.

How could the finance organization have prevented this situation? It could have taken a role when implementing a seemingly nonfinancial application such as logistics. Also, the finance organization should have done what it does best by walking through the logistics processes, focusing on transaction recognition or entry recording. Finance could have established a plan to monitor the new application and caught the issue earlier. All these postmortem actions open up only if finance actively participates.

In today's world of high technology and integrated systems, the finance and accounting roles must grow with the innovations. In the past, finance and accounting focused on recording, reporting, and audit support—all reactive positions. Now, with ERP, most of the recording and reporting has become mundane. Therefore, finance and accounting need to move beyond their traditional role as scorekeepers and understand the relationships of operation processes and finance. In addition, finance and accounting must recognize that technology is no longer just the domain of the information system organization. Finance and accounting need to be technology proficient to comprehend the relationship of process, data, and financial impact. This understanding will require finance and accounting to branch out and actively engage in defining new business processes, because each process will have thousands of transactions run through it—each with a financial impact.

(b) CULTURE OF ORGANIZATIONAL STRUCTURE. In larger finance and accounting organizations, subfunctions are divided by specialties (tax, cost accounting, receivables, payables, asset management, international accounting, etc.). As a way to manage priorities to increase efficiency, each group sets its scope on its specific specialty.

We allow these issues to leave our department relying on the next guy to put the pieces together. Corporate America has right-sized the organization to the point where people can barely complete their own work. We are too focused on our direct responsibilities and usually that in itself consumes all of our time. With organizations that lived through the streamlining of business process reengineering, Six Sigma Quality, right-sizing through shared service deployments, and the most recent savings gained from outsourcing, the average accounting and finance department is now understaffed and more intently focused on its job. Ultimately, this focuses responsibilities immediately in scope, knowing that there could be severe repercussions downstream.

The mixture of this environment and lean company culture creates a silo view of business process, but technology platforms supporting process-based operations create a dichotomy of polar forces. One may lose sight of the whole process and its interdependency. Enterprise application implementation in manufacturing or marketing will not affect finance because that department just owns the back-end processes. Yet, today's systems require end-to-end process focus; thus, gaps result even with enterprise transformation projects using CRM and ERP.

Organizational structure and goals must also change to support the end-to-end focus. Successful organizations have key groups within their organization that focus on the whole process, owning the definition of business process and representing the various information needs of their respective composite functions.

(c) ERROR HANDLING. Another example of the need for cross-functional or holistic process focus is error handling. Particularly in implementing CRM and ERP systems, errors occur that require multiple functions to address. However, the truth is not so obvious, resulting in longer fix times, poor customer experience, and higher costs.

Revenue is significantly lower than planned. Accounting error? Shipping error? Sales error? System error? When researched by department, accounting finds that the revenue agrees with the sales journals and confirms that your figures significantly deviated from your expectations. Shipping/distribution reports that the number of units shipped seem to meet or exceed shipping goals. Sales reports orders on par with goal, but the ledger does not reflect the revenue. The IT department reports no outages or known error directly related to lost revenue.

This example demonstrates the need for a joint cross-functional team to research and help solve the issues. When representatives across each of the various functions begin to work together, the answer becomes quite evident. Why do we wait for these issues to interrupt our business?

Active participation by the functions, including finance and accounting, during the process design and implementation can create the mechanism and culture to prevent and quickly resolve complex relational issues arising from today's systems.

Creation of a process oversight group across the various departments for a particular business process establishes structure and culture for cross-functional teaming. Organizations have created these groups as support functions in IT that own the process and system knowledge. However, it is too frequent that each of the departments contributes inexperienced resources that lack either business knowledge, political savvy, or capabilities to successfully lead the business.

41B.4 WHAT CAN YOU DO?

(a) PARTICIPATE ACTIVELY FROM THE BEGINNING. Understanding the business objective and strategy, this technology implementation is meant to enable revenue enhancement, reduce costs, or bring the company into legal and statutory compliance. Even from a finance perspective, careful review of timing, size, and scope of a potential deployment is required. Benefits of a project, including efficiency and competitive advantage, should be closely weighed against the company's ability to handle the change and deployment timing. Various factors come into play when trying to determine the size of a project a company can handle:

- Experience with enterprise-wide change and the effects it can have on people
- Project management skills related to large-scale projects
- Numbers of competing initiatives and their relative priority
- Impact on the company should the project change scope, last longer than expected, or create short-term unforeseen challenges

(b) FIND A GUIDE—DON'T GO IT ALONE. After the scope and size of the project has been worked out, companies should seek the advice and experience of those who have been down the road before. Avenues a company can explore for advice include:

- System integrators
- Strategists
- Tax and audit professionals
- Software vendors
- Reference customers of various service and software vendors
- Trading partners

The lessons that these companies' experiences can bring to your project are invaluable and can provide hidden gems of information even for the most seasoned project manager and team. Many companies perform this type of investigation early on in a project life cycle, but this effort should be repeated at a minimum for each major phase of the project. (Deployment is no exception—the largest number of pitfalls and their corresponding risk mitigations are encountered during the deployment phase.) The effort to combat these risks should be discussed throughout the project, especially during the deployment phase.

(c) DEVISE A METHOD TO COMMUNICATE AND INTEGRATE. Once the business strategy and the related operation changes by area become apparent, the need will become a matter of integrations. Four key areas are as follows:

1. *Organization.* Alignment of the various participating organizations around the compelling business case to change will facilitate

the integration of project efforts. Departments and organizations within the company should be allowed to develop their own reasons for change and be made champions of project-enabled enhancements.

2. *Process.* Design should include and be structured around the entire end-to-end business process, allowing each function to not only play its part but understand the interdependencies along with the upstream and downstream impacts. Focus on the business process will ensure continuity and facilitate communication.
3. *Data.* Answer the question of who owns and who uses this information. This will help properly align the organizational responsibilities in the process design. Articulate the key business drivers for the data capture, as well as the reporting requirements of various organizations and maintenance goals, and clarify the roles for organizational changes.
4. *Communication.* Communication is the single thread that unites and aligns the top three integration areas. A project- and company-wide communication structure should be developed and owned by a project management, change management, or communication-specific team for the project.

41B.5 CONCLUSION

Enterprise-wide projects can be extremely beneficial and extremely risky for companies to undertake. However, the long-term benefit and return on investment can far outweigh the properly managed risk. The biggest thing to remember when undertaking a large project is that you are not alone. Companies across the globe are implementing and changing their enterprise applications. Do your homework and learn from their experiences. Finally, data and process impact will touch every part of your business, especially finance. Enable communication throughout your organization and increase the finance involvement in every business process.

Index